After the Girls Club

After the Girls Club

How Teenaged Holocaust
Survivors Built New Lives
in America

CAROLE BELL FORD

LEXINGTON BOOKS
A Division of
ROWMAN & LITTLEFIELD PUBLISHERS, INC.
Lanham • Boulder • New York • Toronto • Plymouth, UK

Published by Lexington Books
A division of Rowman & Littlefield Publishers, Inc.
A wholly owned subsidiary of The Rowman & Littlefield Publishing Group, Inc.
4501 Forbes Boulevard, Suite 200, Lanham, Maryland 20706
http://www.lexingtonbooks.com

Estover Road, Plymouth PL6 7PY, United Kingdom

Copyright © 2010 by Lexington Books

British Library Cataloguing in Publication Information Available

Library of Congress Cataloging-in-Publication Data

Ford, Carole Bell, 1934–
  After the Girls Club : how teenaged Holocaust survivors built new lives in America /
Carole Bell Ford.
     p. cm.
  Includes bibliographical references and index.
  ISBN 978-0-7391-4606-4 (cloth : alk. paper) — ISBN 978-0-7391-4608-8 (electronic)
  1. Jewish women—New York (State)—New York—Biography. 2. Holocaust survivors—
New York (State)—New York—Biography. 3. Jews, Polish—New York (State)—New
York—Biography. 4. Women immigrants—New York (State)—New York—Biography.
5. Jewish girls—New York (State)—New York—Biography. 6. Girls Club of Brooklyn—
Biography. 7. Brooklyn (New York, N.Y.)—Biography. 8. Jewish children in the
Holocaust—Poland—Biography. 9. Jewish girls—Poland—Biography. 10. Jews—
Poland—Biography. I. Title.
  F128.9.J5F63 2010
  940.53'180922—dc22
   [B]   2010010701

Printed in the United States of America

For the women of the Girls Club,

and for the other children who survived . . . and thrived.

Contents

A Meeting with Holocaust Survivors—1951 [at the Girls Club]
Cynthia Kohut Himmelfarb

We sat, fidgeting, waiting,
Casting glances at each other
But not wanting our eyes to meet.
Some laughed, forcing jocularity into their tone.
An aura of expectation, dread and uncertainty
Hovered over the room.

Three holocaust survivors had
Agreed to tell their stories.
Three girls in their early 20's
Just like us, their audience,
Were letting us glimpse the horrors
They had lived not so long ago.

How should we respond?
Should we gasp, cry out, sit silently?
Shall we ask questions?
Should we weep?
How does one listen to horror
Told as a tale worthy of Poe
Knowing that Poe could never dream of such terrors?

"After I escaped from the slave labor camp" said one, "I ran for the farmer's field nearby. I lay down deep inside the piles of animal manure, where I knew the guards would not want to look for me. I still think cow shit is the best perfume," she said, with a bitter laugh.

All the stories had the same quality
Leaving us, the protected safe audience with a
Fascination to know more and yet
Hear nothing further.

Many years later the stories have faded.
But the image of a young woman
Digging what could either be a crib, or a grave
In the piles of animal dung
Remains with me.
Always a beacon of faith, hope,
And survival

Preface and Acknowledgments

Until recently our common sense, confirmed by early Holocaust literature, told us that child survivors were injured beyond repair. But as a dear mentor once cautioned me, "common sense tells us the world is flat." In fact, as we have learned more about the lives of young survivors we've come to realize that the most adverse experiences, even the unimaginable horrors of the Holocaust, do not inevitably lead to permanent personality damage. The small group of teenaged survivors whose stories are told here, young women whose lives intersected after World War II at a place called the Girls Club of Brooklyn, are living proof.

I learned about the Girls Club and the women who lived there, between 1946 and 1951, from a friend of theirs who asked if I might be interested in writing their personal histories. It has been my privilege to do so; this is their book. I simply tried to render a faithful account of how they were able to recover from massive loss and trauma, and to reconstruct their lives: to marry and build new families, to nurture their children, to pursue careers outside the home, to find creative outlets—and to pass the wisdom they acquired on to their grandchildren and great-grandchildren. Even now, as they are approaching or are in their eighties, the women continue to be positive about life. They are still future oriented, able to be optimistic, to be grateful, to forgive, to be empathetic. They are able to engage with friends, to trust, to allow new people—such as me—into their lives.

In order to reconstruct their life histories, I interviewed the women over a period of more than five years. Without their participation there would be no book. They are: Betty (Bronka Silvering) Berman; Betty (Basia Pasternak) Ratchik; Doris (Dorka Izbicka) Wasserman; Fran (Frania Dajcz) Berlin; Irma (Stermer) Sangiamo; Lucy (Lusia Bergman) Pasternak; and Renee (Renia Felber) Milchberg. We spoke many times, in person or by phone, and we communicated via post and e-mail.

I would also like to thank others who filled in important missing pieces of the story: Cynthia Kohut Himmelfarb, Shirley Troutman Pouget, Ruth Schwab Georgiou, Sylvia Hoffman, and Larry Ginensky. In addition, I couldn't have reconstructed Sonia (Labiner) Zeigler's story without Philip Zeigler's help.

There is no way to say adequately how much I appreciate the encouragement I received, very early on, from two noted Holocaust scholars, Myrna Goldenberg and Nechama Tec, whom I'd met at a conference in Poland. I was a newcomer to Holocaust studies and was learning what others who came to the subject before me had learned. The life history of a Holocaust survivor is intricate, complex, and full of contradictions. It challenges your convictions about the value of oral history and, at the same time, confirms its value. And it is inevitably transformative as it makes you come to terms with sometimes long-held beliefs about how we define normalcy, about how tragedy is ennobling, about human nature itself.

There were others who offered their ideas and support throughout this project: my good friend Robert Polito; my first readers, Karen Solomon, Myra Sorin, and Martha Tait-Watkins; and Sally MacGillivray, a friend of more than forty years. Sally edited, helpfully suggested changes to the manuscript, and found countless errors that I never would have seen.

Finally, I want to express my profound gratitude to my husband, Steve Ford. He encouraged me to continue with the project when I had my most serious reservations and doubts. When I felt that hearing and retelling the women's Holocaust experiences was just too difficult, he admonished me: "If they lived through it," he said, "can you say it's too hard for you to write about it?"

1

Introduction

The Women and the Girls Club

I found people with my background, my interests, like myself. I made friendships for life.

—*Fran (Frania Dajcz) Berlin*

Betty Berman and I are sitting in the living room of her home in Minneapolis, close to the west bank of the Mississippi River. The room is smartly furnished: full of artwork—sculpture, pottery, paintings—yet very comfortable. Betty's eyes sparkle. She has a mischievous, youthful energy that belies her age of almost eighty years. But at this moment she is somber, remembering something so incongruous in this relaxed setting it seemed surreal. Betty—in Poland her name was Bronka—had arrived in Auschwitz. It was August 1944. She was fifteen, bewildered, disoriented. "I couldn't understand why I was in hell. How had this happened? Why had it happened?"

It is possible, of course, to trace the roots and expression of viral anti-Semitism through the centuries and it is possible to reconstruct the execution of Nazi policy in much of its horrifying detail. Many historians have traced the evolution of the Holocaust: Hitler's war against the Jews, or what came to be known as the "Final Solution to the Jewish question."[1] Still, the haunting questions Betty asks are confounding on the deepest human level and have remained unresolved, despite the accumulated wisdom of a massive scholarship, for more than sixty-five years. Nor does this small volume presume to answer Betty's questions.

This book is not an analysis of the Holocaust. Its purpose is to tell the life histories of a small group of young women who survived, as all survivors did, against almost insuperable odds: women whose life choices were subsequently informed, if not defined, by the common macabre backdrop of the Holocaust. At the same time, this book presents more than a collective, personal history. Because these women exemplify the broad range of experiences that Jews suffered, during and after the Holocaust, their stories—elaborated with relevant information about places, people, events, and issues—are also the stories of tens of thousands of child survivors. Collectively, the women experienced life in the ghettos, in slave labor and concentration camps, in hiding, with the partisans, in exile in the outermost reaches of the Soviet Union (Siberia, Kazakhstan, Uzbekistan), and in refugee camps after the war ended. Yet the Holocaust is just the beginning. As the women's life histories continue in America they become stories of recovery and of renewal.

Like Betty, the women, mostly from Poland, are among the relatively small number of child survivors of the Holocaust. They were children—eight, nine, or ten years old when the war began—and teenagers when it ended. And, as the result of a coincidence of history and geography, they share another uncommon bond. For a few brief years, far from the devastation that was Europe after World War II, these orphaned teens, bereaved and bewildered, had the good fortune to find a safe haven in a place with an unassuming name, the Girls Club of Brooklyn—not actually a club at all but, rather, a residence for young Jewish women. The Girls Club was where the young women's devastating physical and psychological wounds began to heal and where their new lives began.

I learned about the Girls Club as a result of a chance meeting with a woman, a Holocaust survivor, who had spent most of the war in Siberia. She met Sonia, one of the residents, at Thomas Jefferson High School in Brownsville, Brooklyn, where they were enrolled in a program in English language and culture that was offered for recently-arrived immigrant teenagers; subsequently, she became friends with Sonia and with some of the other girls. She offered to help me contact them if I was interested in telling their stories.

I was very interested. At the very least, telling the women's stories would be an opportunity to add to the literature of witness testimony. The record is still incomplete, and time is running out; the very youngest Holocaust survivors are now in their late sixties. But there were other issues that interested me as well. These women were children in 1939 when the war began, teenagers when it ended. At an especially vulnerable stage in their development they had to cope with extreme and long-lasting trauma. Now they are approaching or are in their eighties. In old age the women are, once again, going through one of the most challenging periods in their lives, a time that can be exceptionally and uniquely difficult for Holocaust survivors. Consequently, while exploring the full scope of the women's life stories is worthwhile in itself, their early and late years warrant particular scrutiny. For instance, what was the link between their early experiences and their decisions as young, and later mature, adults? Could they see and articulate a connection? Now that they are elderly, how are they coping with the stresses of old age? Do their experiences confirm what the literature on aging—and aging women, aging survivors, and especially aging child survivors—tells us? I wanted to examine these and many other issues.

When the women came to America, some brought the few mementos they had managed to hold onto through their perilous journey; above all, they brought their precious memories of life before the carnage. They also brought a substantial emotional and psychological *pekl*, the Yiddish term that Lucy, one of the women, uses to conjure the image of a heavy weight. It was at the Girls Club that they began to unburden themselves and their wounded psyches began to mend. There they regained their physical strength; they began to glue the bits of their fragmented lives back together. Once the healing began they moved on to construct new and successful lives, as success is defined for women of their generation and social class. Today, in contrast with what much of the earlier literature predicted about how survivors would cope—particularly child survivors—the women continue to make the best of the lives they rebuilt for themselves, even into old age.

In a newspaper article, writer Daniel Mendelsohn describes an incident that occurred when he was interviewing a Holocaust survivor for his book *The Lost: A Search for Six of the Six Million.* "What an amazing story," Mendelsohn remarked when a woman told him how she and her son had survived the war. "'Amazing story,'" she responded dismissively. "'If you didn't have an amazing story, you didn't survive'" (2008, n.p.). So it is with this history; each woman's account of her experiences is amazing, is compelling, and wants to be told. Each story is unique while at the same time a variation on a theme—a grotesque theme, a shared nightmare.

Immediately before they came to America, still in their teens, these young women were classified as displaced persons, DPs—the abbreviation that has become so familiar that we need to remind ourselves that it means dislodged, disordered, disrupted, dislocated. Four were survivors of the ghettos and camps. Two had been in hiding, one had found refuge in the woods with partisans, and another had been sent to the farthest reaches, the *stans* of the Soviet Union.[2] They were orphans, traumatized and exceptionally needy, looking for a home. They were, as other survivors have been described, "desolate—lonely, not merely in the way people are who are new to a country but in the deeper way of those who have suddenly had withdrawn from them some elemental connection in life" (Rabinowitz, 1976, p. 105).

As children, the women "suffered the unique trauma of being condemned to total extermination" (Sternberg & Rosenbloom, 2000, p. 6). Although exact numbers are not known there may have been as few as 100,000 Jewish child survivors in all; it is estimated that only about 11 percent survived the war (Dwork, 1991, p. xi). Out of approximately 1.6 million Jewish children who were alive in countries under Nazi control in 1939, 1.5 million were killed. In Poland, the women were among only 5,000 who survived out of 1 million Jewish children who were alive at the beginning of the war (Plight, 2009, paras. 1 and 8). Whether in the camps or in hiding, as children and young teenagers the women were subjected to fear, humiliation, extreme privation, and illness. They lost their parents and grandparents; most lost their siblings, some lost their entire extended families as well. The "lucky" ones found a family member alive after the war—a brother or sister, an aunt or cousin. Most of the women languished in DP camps for several years until they were relocated to America by HIAS (the Hebrew Immigrant Aid Society), UNRRA (the United Nations Relief and Rehabilitation Administration),[3] or other organizations that had been set up for that purpose after the war. When they arrived, the teenagers lived with relatives with whom they had come to America, or with aunts or uncles who had emigrated before the war. For various reasons each girl could not, or chose not, to remain with her relative. That was when she was placed, usually by her social worker, at the Girls Club.

The history of the Girls Club can be traced back to the late nineteenth century, when the Brooklyn Hebrew Orphan Asylum (BHOA) was granted a state charter. BHOA "invested $500" in a house large enough for sixteen children in what is now the Bedford-Stuyvesant section of what was still the city of Brooklyn, soon to become a borough of New York City (Bernard, 1972, p. 15). It wasn't until 1915 that the organization, actually the "wives of BHOA trustees," founded the Girls Club (Bernard, 1972, p. 89). By the late 1940s, when the young women in this history settled into their rooms at the Girls Club, it was housed in a different area (today known as Prospect Heights) in a five-story building much like hundreds of others that were built earlier in the century. The building was in a great location. At 174 Prospect Place, it was close to Prospect Park and the Brooklyn Botanic Garden, the Brooklyn Museum, and the main branch of the Brooklyn Public Library at Grand Army Plaza. It was a short walk to the subway stations with connections to Manhattan and the other boroughs of New York City. In 1949, after a brief period of overcrowding, the Girls Club was home to about thirty Jewish "girls," young women in their late teens and early twenties (Bernard, 1972, p. 134).

Only a small number of the Girls Club residents were *greener*, as they called themselves. It was a term used by Yiddish speakers and derived from "greenhorn," a self-mocking reference to newly-arrived immigrants. Most of the residents were native-born Americans who came to New York from all over the country to work or to go to school. Some came because they lived in small towns where there were few Jewish boys they could marry. A few American girls, such as sisters Shirley and Audrey Troutman, found shelter from troubled or abusive homes. Others, like the Europeans, were orphans. When Cynthia Kohut's mother died, her father couldn't care for her or her brother. She came to the Girls Club from an orphanage in Brooklyn where she'd lived for six years, and at least one other American resident at that time had lived in orphanages all of her life.[4]

All but one of the European girls was from Poland, which meant that this subgroup could reconstitute a tiny community. The members, Lucy says, "understood each other"—not simply because they had a common language but because, as they correctly believed, those who had not experienced the Holocaust could not comprehend what they'd endured no matter how empathetic they might have been. The girls also provided each other with much-needed continuity with their lost world since, like other Holocaust survivors, they were "not only without a place in the world and without possessions but also had no past life; the roots and ties to that life . . . had been erased entirely" (Rabinowitz, 1976, p. 107). The girls became each other's one link with the past. Of course, they couldn't replace lost parents, grandparents, siblings—they were, after all, only teenagers—but they were a bridge. They knew the old world and were part of the new.

Who were these young women, the *greener*, who lived at the Girls Club?

Betty (Basia) Pasternak was the youngest, only seven years old when the war began. In 1949, she was also one of the last of the group to come to America after the war, and to the Girls Club. In the earliest days of the war, Betty and her family were sent to the ghetto in her home town of Tarnopol in Galicia, a region near Poland's eastern border with the Soviet Union. Her parents and her older brother arranged for her to be hidden, and she remained there until the town was "liberated" by the Soviet army. Betty's parents didn't survive the war; she was brought to America by her older brother and sister.

Lucy (Lusia) Bergman is one of three women in the group who grew up in Lodz and lived in the ghetto there during most of the war, from 1939 to 1944. When it was "liquidated" (the term commonly used to describe such an event) the members of her family who had not succumbed to the ghetto's brutality were sent to Auschwitz. Only Lucy, her mother, and her mother's youngest sister survived. The three women were sent from Auschwitz to a slave-labor mining camp in Germany and, from there, they were force-marched to Bergen-Belsen where they spent the remainder of the war. Ultimately, Lucy's mother did not survive.

Betty (Bronka) Silvering was born in Germany but grew up in Lodz. Betty and Lucy didn't know each other although they were the same age, had spent most of the war in the Lodz ghetto, and were then sent to Auschwitz. At that point their paths diverged. Betty's mother was killed in Auschwitz, but her mother's sister survived. From Auschwitz, Betty and her aunt were sent to a work camp near Dresden. They were still in Dresden at the time of the notorious fire bombing in 1945. Betty and Lucy finally met at the Girls Club.

Doris (Dorka) Izbicka also grew up in Lodz. In a coincidence that seems so contrived it would be ridiculed if it were fiction, Doris and Lucy, schoolmates and childhood friends in Lodz, were reunited at the Girls Club. They hadn't seen each other since their families were sent to the ghetto. From the ghetto,

Doris was sent to Auschwitz, then to a labor camp, and from there to Mauthausen, a notorious concentration camp. Orphaned, Doris came to America with a surviving brother and sister.

Fran (Frania) Dajcz grew up in Pabianice, a small town near Lodz. She had been living in a series of rented rooms before she came to the Girls Club. When Lucy saw her, she experienced another coincidence, almost as astonishing as her reunion with Doris. Fran and Lucy hadn't met in the Lodz ghetto, to which Fran's family had been sent from her hometown. But the girls did meet when they followed the same torturous route from Lodz to Auschwitz, to the same mining camp and from there, via a forced march, to Bergen-Belsen. Fran lost all of her immediate and most of her extended family in the war.

Sonia Labiner lived in a small village in Galicia, Premyshlany, until her family was removed to a nearby ghetto. When her mother learned that the ghetto was going to be liquidated she sent Sonia—then twelve years old—to hide in the forest. Her parents and siblings were subsequently killed. But Sonia eventually met up with Jewish partisans and spent the remainder of the war with them (Kleinberg, 1980, p. 98).[5] She was a central and charismatic figure at the Girls Club.

Renee (Renia) Felber, who was from Sanok, another town in Galicia, spent most of the war in Siberia and Uzbekistan. Renee was caught up in one of the lesser known chapters of the Holocaust story. Because the Soviet Union and Germany had agreed upon a division of Poland in their prewar pact, Renee ended up on the "Russian side" in the care of an aunt and uncle. Like many Jewish and non-Jewish Poles who found themselves under Soviet control early in the war, they were deported to a work camp in Siberia.

Irma Stermer's experiences were different from the other girls'. She was born in a small town in Austria. After that country was annexed by Germany, Irma's mother arranged for her to be taken away from the Vienna ghetto, where the family had been relocated, to the relative safety of a children's home in France. Two years later, when Jewish children in France had to flee from the Nazis, Irma was sent to America. When she graduated from high school, Irma moved from her foster home to the Girls Club. She was one of the first of the Europeans refugees to live there after the war.

There were a number of other Holocaust survivors living at the Girls Club during the same period as these women. A few of the women I contacted refused, for various reasons, to participate in this project; some even refused to speak with me. It's been noted that one reason survivors refuse to talk about their experiences is that they're suspicious of the motives of outsiders. I had one such encounter. When I telephoned a friend of Renee's, another former Girls Club resident, her husband answered the phone. I explained why I was calling. He hesitated a moment, then said, "Obviously, you're trying to make a buck off of the bones of Holocaust victims." His wife, he told me, wouldn't want to speak with me. He was right about that. She did come to the phone, but only to tell me that she had nothing to say; she hung up as I was in mid-sentence. I was disappointed, yet I could understand their cynicism and fear of exploitation.

One woman I telephoned didn't want to take part in the study, she said, because she was in the process of writing her own memoir. If she does, it will add to the important and steadily growing body of Holocaust memoir literature. Another, one of the first women I met with, had been interviewed a number of times before; she'd been on the radio, taped, quoted in some publications. It seemed to me, as happens with oft-repeated stories, a script had evolved that she was able to recite, almost by rote. When I probed she seemed reluctant to elaborate; she said that some of my questions were naïve. But she became hostile when I tried to explore some gender issues. She subsequently told me, when I attempted to make a follow-up appointment, that her primary identification was not as a woman in the Holocaust. Consequently, she was not interested in being included in the study. If the topic of gender differences in the Holocaust was, indeed, the reason she dropped out of the study, she is not alone in her antagonism. Holocaust-related gender studies continue to be a contentious subject among many Holocaust survivors and scholars; while they may allow that women and men experienced the Holocaust differently, they believe that focusing on gender dilutes the importance of the primary issues of anti-Semitism and genocide.[6]

Some of the women, those who did agree to recount their experiences for me—Lucy, for one—were, nevertheless, quite cautious. At our first meeting Lucy set the boundaries; she was happy to talk about the Girls Club but she wouldn't talk about the Holocaust. Yet as the women, including Lucy, came to trust me more, they shared more and more of their experiences and feelings. Some had not spoken about their wartime experiences with anyone since the Girls Club, not even with their children, which is not uncommon among Ho-

locaust survivors. I wanted to be flattered, to believe I'm simply a brilliant interviewer who was able to draw them out. But I think otherwise; I believe the
women were responding, without realizing it, to a need to tell their stories.

Judith Herman, who has studied post-traumatic stress among Holocaust
survivors, writes that the "will to deny horrible events" finds its equal in the
"will to proclaim them aloud." This conflict, Herman says, is the "central
dialectic" in response to trauma. She explains: "The ordinary response to
atrocities is to banish them from consciousness. Certain violations of the
social compact are too terrible to utter aloud: this is the meaning of the word
unspeakable. Atrocities, however, refuse to be buried. Equally as powerful
as the desire to deny atrocities is the conviction that denial does not work"
(1992, p. 1).

Not only for the benefit of the historical record but also for the survivors'
own good, it is to be hoped that the need to remember and to tell "the truth
about terrible events" will predominate since it is necessary "for the healing
of the individual victims" (Herman, 1992, p. 1). We have come to understand
that life storytelling can bridge the gulf between what seems a surreal past
and today's reality; it is one way of making sense of that past, distinguishing it
from the present but at the same time recognizing that the past "extends into
the present" (Rosenthal, 2003, p. 927). In telling their life stories, survivors
can bring their traumatic experiences into the larger narrative, see how they
fit, and accept them as an essential part of the whole. The need to tell the
stories can be prompted by an interviewer, but it originates within the psyche
of the storyteller. It seems I was a catalyst, particularly for those women who
had resisted talking about their experiences before, even with their children.
Doris surprised me, and herself even more, when a rather innocuous question
prompted a floodgate of memories. Her reaction was, almost verbatim, one
that others have expressed to a number of different interviewers (Rosenthal,
2003, p. 925): "What did you do to me to make me tell all of this?"

I am not a therapist, however. And while I hope that relating their stories
was helpful to Doris and the other women, my intention was simply to hear
and retell their histories as faithfully as I could. I know, however, that the
goal of arriving at a factually correct and complete reconstruction of events,
despite a most sincere attempt, can be easily compromised by a number of
factors. Some of the issues that confound an accurate retelling relate to the
storyteller herself, others to the interviewer, and still others concern the

process. Is it even possible to uncover the truth (that is, objective truth) about such intense, complex, traumatic experiences, ones so colored by emotion? The literature tells us that memory is notoriously unreliable for trauma victims—and the younger they were, and the more traumatized they were, the more unreliable. In addition, there are major issues related to memory over the passage of time. Can stories be accurate reconstructions of events that occurred sixty years before?[7]

Early on, I came upon an interesting incongruence in the stories of the reunion of Lucy and Doris at the Girls Club. Lucy arrived in America in 1946. She had been here for two years and had just graduated from high school when she came to live at the Girls Club. The director of the residence, Mrs. Feldman, took Lucy to see her room and to meet her roommates. She was introduced to Natalie, an American girl. Her other roommate was out, working perhaps, Lucy isn't sure. But a large framed photo of her—"she was very beautiful," Lucy says—was on the bureau. She walked over to look at it more closely: "Yes," Lucy thought, "she does look familiar." As Lucy examined the photo more intently, she began to make an adjustment in her mind. Then she stopped: "I was frozen. I couldn't believe it!" Lucy was looking into the face of her childhood friend, Doris. How could it be possible, she thought? "How could we meet again, here, after all we'd been through—in Brooklyn, in the Girls Club, in another world?"

Doris's recollection of meeting Lucy in the Girls Club, however, is different from Lucy's. Doris doesn't remember the photograph. They disagree about who first came to live at the Girls Club, who first came upon the other, and the nature of the encounter. Doris says: "Lucy was at the Girls Club before me. I remember it distinctly, as if it were yesterday. When I came there, I saw her in a room, *davening* (praying in a typically Jewish manner) and I recognized her immediately. I was shocked because we never were religious when we lived in Poland."

Lucy thinks Doris must be remembering her in the room they shared at the Girls Club, reciting the *Sh'ma* (a daily prayer):[8] "I always said it every night, before I went to bed." Doris concedes that they did room together, but later on. As Kurosawa depicted in the classic film, *Rashomon*, eyewitnesses to the same event tell different versions of the same story, each certain that their version is true. Lucy and Doris remember their first encounter quite differently from each other, and each woman is sure that her version is correct.[9]

This simple example illustrates at least two important points: the details often conflict, yet the larger story remains intact. There is no doubt that Lucy and Doris met at the Girls Club after not having seen each other since their families were sent to the ghetto early in the war, the reunion the result of a remarkably unpredictable set of circumstances. There are some other differing descriptions of common experiences among the women who lived in the Girls Club, some conflicting stories, even contradictions within an individual's own account. But when the women's answers to a particular question were the same, independent of each other, they validated each other's perceptions. Most important, the women all agree on the key points so that, taken together, they confirm the truth of the larger picture.

With the proliferation of memoirs and survivor testimony it is now understood, as with the story of Lucy and Doris's meeting, that what used to be treated as "unalloyed truth" has been shaped by memory (Baer & Goldenberg, 2003, p. xv). When survivors tell their stories, they do not merely describe events. Inevitably, as all storytellers do, they construct their narratives. Consequently, "historical records cannot and are not built on survivor testimony alone" (Lewin, 1990, p. 218). Yet survivor testimony is valued: "It remains an important source of information, however many shortcomings it has. The details may be flawed but they verify the historical record—they were in the ghetto, in the camps. They refute those who, still, after all the information and representation that has been amassed, deny that the Holocaust occurred, or at the very least, claim that it is an exaggeration (Lewin, 1990, p. 218).

Important as they are in verifying the historical record, memoirs, witness testimony, and personal histories such as this one serve additional purposes. For example, as Baer and Goldenberg wrote about essayists (in *Experience and Expression*) who studied "particular women in particular locations, particular roles and behaviors, particular memories and representations," it is "through such particularities" that we are able to arrive at a greater understanding (2003, p. 2). One reason is that the small picture sharpens the focus; individual accounts of the Holocaust "permit us to imagine how it must have felt in human terms" (Lewin, 1990, p. xiii). They transform historical incidents into personal, intimate stories, enabling us to identify with those involved. One of the most obvious examples is the diary of Anne Frank. The intimacy, the detail of the memoir or eyewitness account, breaks through the barriers we have built to emotionally insulate ourselves from the horrors and personal tragedies. It is why life stories such as those depicted in film and theater are so moving. It is why a film such as *The Pianist* enables us to empathize with those who were caught up in the events of the Warsaw ghetto.

Six million is an impossible number to comprehend.[10] One and a half million, the number of Jewish children who were killed in the Holocaust, is equally overwhelming to imagine. The collective life history presented in this book is one effort to reduce what is incomprehensible in its abstraction to a manageable size.

The women's stories provide yet another intense lesson, one in absolutes and relativity. Take, for instance, the relative meaning of "luck." Imagine how your perception of that notion is altered when a woman tells you, referring to the others, "I was blessed; I didn't suffer as much as the others." The woman, Renee, considers herself fortunate for having spent the war years in the remote and hostile lands in the farthest reaches of the Soviet Union, in an alien environment, living barely one degree above that of a prisoner of war. Early in the war, as the result of a Soviet-Nazi agreement, Renee's town was divided between the two invading forces. Her mother took Renee across the temporary border of the town, Sanok, to what she believed was safety on the "Russian side," and left her in the care of friends. Her mother went back for Renee's sister, but she never returned. Except for the aunt and uncle with whom she was subsequently transported to Siberia, Renee lost all of her family. Still, she considers herself one of the lucky ones at the Girls Club. She was not "*in* the Holocaust" like the other girls.

Irma tells a different story. But, like Renee, she never thought of herself as a Holocaust survivor despite the fact that she lost almost her entire family. When Austria was annexed to Germany in March 1938, in what is known as the *Anschluss*, all Austrian Jews were sent to ghettoes. Somehow, Irma's mother arranged to get her out of the country, to a children's refuge in France. Today we know that many "courageous parents," like Irma's mother, sent their children away even though they were taking "the risk of never seeing their children again" (Bluegrass, 2003, p. 14). Since it was still early in the war, perhaps Irma's mother dared to think that Irma would be kept safe and would return home when it was over, a logical assumption at that time. Even after the escalation of Jewish persecution and the series of anti-Semitic events of the 1930s, even after Jews' and others' civil rights were curtailed, even after the destruction of *Kristallnacht*,[11] who could have conceived of the mass extermination of European Jewry? Before it occurred, back in that historical time, even the most informed who took Hitler's ravings seriously could not have conceived of the Holocaust.

Irma spent two years in a children's home in France. Then, in 1941, she was brought to New York on the *Serba Pinta*, the third and last of the children's transports to arrive in the States before America entered the war. Irma had been sent away from her home when she was ten years old, separated from and never to be reunited with her family. But, like Renee, Irma believes she was a lucky one; she didn't suffer like the others, like most of the Polish girls. In part, Irma didn't think of herself as a survivor of the Holocaust since the perception, common in the early days of Holocaust studies, was that survivors were only those who endured slave labor or concentration camps. Others—who had been in hiding, who joined the resistance or partisans, or had escaped to other countries, or had been sent to Siberia—didn't fit the category of "Holocaust survivor." More recently the definition of survivor has been extended to include people like Irma and Renee.

Cynthia Kohut, one of the young American women who lived at the Girls Club during the time of this history, wrote a poem about an event that was held there in 1951, when three survivors agreed to share their stories. In her poem, reproduced in its entirety in the front pages of this volume, Cynthia wrote:

> All the stories had the same quality
> Leaving us, the protected safe audience with a
> Fascination to know more and yet
> Hear nothing further.

Like Cynthia and many others, I admit that over the years I've resisted hearing more about the Holocaust than I had to. Yet, as an educated person, a historian, and also a Jew, I thought I was reasonably well informed. It was tempting to think, as I did: "Well, I guess I've heard the worst of the stories now." But then I would hear another, even more terrible than the one before, each one forcing me to make an alteration in my evolving concept of the extremes of human behavior, in the ability both to inflict and to tolerate pain, humiliation, suffering, and deprivation. Hearing their stories I not only recognized my ignorance but learned a great deal more than I had set out to learn.

By entering the world of these Holocaust survivors, I believe I did arrive at the greater understanding Baer and Goldenberg anticipated. The reader, too, will find that it is impossible to avoid a deeper and broader understanding of events and circumstances: an understanding that inevitably progresses beyond the intellectual. The women's profoundly affecting stories are transformative; as they challenge previously held assumptions, they force a shift in perception and perspective. Stories such as theirs break through whatever protective shells we may have constructed over the years of hearing about the unfathomable horrors of the Holocaust; they heighten our sensitivities, our ability to empathize.

This collective personal history, *After the Girls Club*, is the story of a handful of children who survived the Holocaust against all odds, and began their lives anew in a caring place—in my own hometown of Brooklyn, New York. It is about their early histories, their years together at the Girls Club, their ability to cope with the extreme trauma they suffered in Europe during and after the Holocaust, their rehabilitated lives, and how they are dealing with the challenges facing them in the last decades of their lives. Lucy believes the Girls Club was the safe haven that enabled her to go on with her life. While not all of the women award the Girls Club quite the importance that she does, they all remember it as an extraordinary place. Though the devil may be in the details, the undeniably larger truth about the Girls Club is that it played a critical role at a critical time in the women's lives. That is their unanimous perception, and it has remained consistent over the years. Fran says, "I found people with my background, my interests, like myself. I made friendships for life."

In order to fully appreciate why the Girls Club represents such a defining moment in the women's lives, it is important to see what their lives were like before the great divide that was the Holocaust. Their stories begin, seventy-odd years ago, in Poland.

NOTES

1. For details regarding the origin of the phrase and concept, see the work of Christopher Browning.

2. It is generally accepted that the suffix *stan* is an ancient Persian or Farsi word meaning place or place of. Until late in the twentieth century, these countries were part of the Soviet Union. They all became independent in 1991 when the U.S.S.R. was dissolved. See USHMM, "Escape from German-Occupied Europe," *Holocaust Encyclopedia.*

3. The Allies chartered the United Nations Relief and Rehabilitation Administration (UNRRA) at a conference at the White House on November 9, 1943. The express purpose of the agency was the repatriation and support of refugees who would come under Allied control at the war's end. In late 1947, its tasks were delegated to its successor agency, the International Refugee Organization (IRO), which undertook similar responsibilities but concentrated more on financial security. The agencies and their officers, including former New York City mayor Fiorello H. La Guardia, who served as UNRRA director general from March 1946 to January 1947, set important precedents for the care of refugees.

4. Telephone interview with social worker Ruth Schwab Georgiou. Cynthia is the author of the poem, "A Meeting with Holocaust Survivors."

5. Seymour Kleinberg (98), a close friend of Sonia's, wrote about her in two memoirs: *Alienated Affections* and *The Fugitive Self.*

6. There will be further discussion of Holocaust-related gender issues.

7. I am not referring to issues of conscious fabrication, such as the recent case of a fictionalized "love story" that duped both its publisher and Oprah Winfrey.

8. The *Sh'ma* is actually an abbreviation for *Sh'ma Yisroel or Shema Yisrael* ("Hear, O Israel") the first two words of a section of the Torah (the Hebrew Bible) that is used as a centerpiece of all morning and evening Jewish prayer services: "Hear, O Israel! The Lord is our God! The Lord is One!" The *Sh'ma* is the most important prayer in Judaism; its twice-daily recitation is a *mitzvah* or religious commandment.

9. When I worked through the time line of arrivals in America and the length of time Doris and Lucy lived elsewhere before they came to the Girls Club, it does seem that Doris was living at the Girls Club before Lucy's arrival there. Yet there is no evidence, no proof, no other witness to these particular events, nor has the agency retained records that could be checked for verification.

10. There is a wonderful program started a few years ago at a rural middle school in Tennessee called the *Paper Clip Project.* It began as an attempt to make the

number of Jewish victims of the Holocaust comprehensible to the young students by collecting one paper clip for each victim, and evolved into something even more meaningful. References can be found on the Internet.

11. *Kristallnacht* means "Crystal Night" or the "Night of Broken Glass." During the nights of November 9 and 10, 1938, almost one hundred Jews were murdered and 25,000 to 30,000 were taken to concentration camps.

Lodz

A Path to the Ghetto

We were only children. It was very scary; we were surrounded by wires. There were soldiers with guns and rifles.

—*Lucy (Lusia Bergman) Pasternak*

Lusia thought life was normal before the Nazi occupation of Poland in 1939. Most of the other women of the Girls Club agree.

Lusia was just ten years old when the occupation began. "All I knew was school and my little girlfriends," she says, "and that I was going to the same gymnasium as my mother went to, and that was my goal." Lusia and Dorka, childhood friends and schoolmates, were blissfully oblivious to some of the worst realities of life in interwar Poland, particularly the escalating, virulent anti-Semitism. "We were too young to realize anti-Semitism," Lusia continued. "We heard about it from our parents but I didn't experience it until some Polish children threw stones at me, just before the war."

Lusia and Dorka played with their friends after school, did their household chores, and took advantage of the usual things there were for middle-class children to do in Lodz. A large and sophisticated city with a large Jewish population—after Warsaw, it had the largest Jewish population in Europe—Lodz was an unusual multicultural mix. Before World War II, approximately one-third were German, one-third were Poles, and the other third, about 240,000 in 1939, were Jews.

In the early nineteenth century, Lodz had grown from a sleepy little village into a prosperous factory town, "a powerful manufacturing center in the European textile industry" (Podolska, 2004b, p. 6). By 1850, the population had increased to 15,000, and by the outbreak of World War I it had exploded to 750,000; the city's leading industrialists were the wealthiest in the Russian Empire. Among them were Jews who lived in grand palaces alongside their Christian peers. Although, by the eve of World War II, Lodz had declined from its heyday when the huge factories were self-contained cities—each with 10,000 workers, housing for their families, schools, and hospitals—a number of factories remained in operation. Lodz Jews still enjoyed a full cultural life: there were Jewish cinemas; theatrical performances were staged in Yiddish; Jews had established private schools and libraries; they had built hospitals; and they had founded numerous and diverse social and political organizations. Of course, there were many synagogues; for the observant, they were the loci of Jewish tradition (Podolska, 2004b, p. 6). It may seem surprising that children such as Lusia, who lived in one of Poland's major cities, could be shielded from anti-Semitism since, quite contrary to her characterization, life for Polish Jews was not at all normal—particularly in the years leading up to the war. But her perception was not unique. As a Schindler's-list survivor from Krakow explained, anti-Semitism "didn't reveal itself in the part of the city" where he lived either (Zuckerman, 1991, p. 9); that is, in the *Kuzemark* district (known as *Kazimierz* in Polish). When he was a young man, the neighborhood was relatively insular, since it was 80 or 90 percent Jewish. It was a voluntary, comfortable ghetto where Jews had their businesses, or to which they could return at the end of the day. Many Polish Jews lived in similar neighborhoods.

Most Jews in Poland were city dwellers, although about a quarter of the Jewish population of Poland lived in *shtetlach*, small villages and towns. In fact, most of the refugees at the Girls Club grew up in *shtetlach* with rhythmical names like Pabianice and Prezemyshlany. In these small towns, Jews often comprised a significant number and, in many, a majority. Since, as in many urban neighborhoods, they had their own schools "and social structure," Jews and Catholic Poles "lived parallel lives with very little contact."[1] Consequently, because there was so little integration in the towns—unless there had been specific attacks or incidents—many *shtetl* children were protected, as many city children like Lusia were, from the ever-increasing ostracism of Jews in interwar Poland.

Not all children, however, were so fortunate. Some Jewish children, and certainly their parents, were well-aware of the dark, anti-Semitic mood of the country. In memoirs, child survivors describe incidents or experiences that occurred in schools, among their non-Jewish friends, or at local shops. Bronka, for example, was unable to remain completely naïve. Like Dorka and Lusia, she lived in Lodz—but in a "tough and poor" neighborhood. She distinctly remembers being afraid of the Polish police and always crossing the street when they approached. She says:

> I was protected from all this bigotry by family and community because I was very young, but not too young to be keenly aware of being "the other." Schools were segregated. Most of my teachers were not Jewish; I remember having one Jewish teacher.
>
> We did live in harmony with some of our non-Jewish neighbors, but others we avoided. I do remember some name calling at playgrounds—I remember walking away from these verbal fights feeling morally superior.

In addition to memoirs, there is a unique resource which provides an understanding of the more sophisticated, if jaded, perceptions held by older youth during this time. In 1932, 1934, and again on the eve of the war in 1939, a series of competitions was sponsored in Poland by the YIVO Institute for Jewish Research. Jewish youth between the ages of sixteen and twenty were invited to write their life histories, to help researchers understand more about their lives. Prizes were awarded for the best-written auto-biographies—150 zlotys, about $30—which, considering the increasing poverty of Jews in this period, was quite enticing. A large number of these autobiographies have survived and provide detailed images of Jewish youth in the interwar period: their experiences, how they understood themselves and their society, their hopes and aspirations, and their frustrations and conflicts. Because many of the writers were quite politically aware, their writing reflects the disappointment over lost opportunities that seemed to have been possible only a decade earlier, at the establishment of the Polish republic. As a result of the overwhelming impact of anti-Semitism, many also describe their despair at living in "a world in which young people found it extraordinarily difficult to find a place for themselves" (Steinlauf, 2002, p. 4).[2]

Anti-Jewish attitudes were not a new phenomenon, of course. They had been part of Polish life since Jews were first permitted to settle in Poland around the middle of the fourteenth century. By that time anti-Jewish sentiment in most of Western Europe had intensified to the point that Jews, consistently blamed for a variety of transgressions and subversions, were even blamed for causing the Black Death by poisoning the wells. Hundreds of Jewish communities were destroyed by violence as massacres spread throughout Spain, France, Germany, and Austria. The more fortunate were expelled, and many Jews found their way to Poland, first settling in the Warsaw area. Despite the anti-Jewish attitudes they encountered in Poland, which were expressed in discrimination and periodic *pogroms* (organized attacks against minority groups, usually Jews), Polish Jews thrived and created a vital community.

By the late nineteenth century, Poland was an important center of Jewish culture, with dynamic writers and intellectuals leading the Jewish renaissance, or *Haskala*. Prior to World War I, there was already a flourishing Yiddish theater, the most famous of which was the Kaminska Theater in Warsaw.[3] In 1925, the YIVO Institute for Jewish Research was founded in Vilna, part of Poland at that time,[4] by European intellectuals, including Albert Einstein and Sigmund Freud. Its early goal was to record the history and culture of Eastern European Jews.

The Jewish press, which had a huge circulation, was published in three languages: Polish, Yiddish, and Hebrew. Poland had no fewer than two dozen Yiddish language dailies and even more weekly newspapers. Jewish-Polish newspapers were read by Jews throughout the world. *Haint* (*Today*)—considered the most important Yiddish newspaper in the world—as well as another mass-circulation paper, *Moment*, were published in Warsaw. The circulation of the Hebrew press was more modest since Hebrew was not the daily language of most Polish Jews.

The large number of newspapers, which represented an enormous philosophical range, also reflected the great diversity among Polish Jews with respect to religion, education, economic class, and political affiliation. There was "a full range—from assimilated Jews in Krakow and Warsaw who were part of the political and social spectrum to Hasidic communities, which were divided following particular teachings of the given rabbi. . . . In the big cities there was always a big assimilated section of the Jewish community, and in political life the Jewish community spanned a whole variety of political ideas from Zionism to Socialism to assimilationist ideas" (Prazmowska, 2001, n.p.).

Language was another indicator of Jewish diversity. As was common among urban, middle-class, educated, assimilated, and secular Jews, Lusia's parents spoke Polish. Her mother was a schoolteacher in a state secondary school (very rare for a Jewish woman in interwar Poland). Lusia learned Yiddish only because her mother worked long hours and Lusia spent most of her after-school time with her Yiddish-speaking maternal grandmother. Among the women of the Girls Club, you can find all the variations of language usage among Polish Jews before the war. Some, like Lusia, spoke Yiddish only with their grandparents. Dorka and Bronka spoke Yiddish only at home, Polish outside the home. Others spoke Polish to their parents at home, while their parents spoke to them in Yiddish.[5]

After World War I, when a Polish republic was reestablished independent of the Russian Empire, it was "heralded by Poles and Jews alike as the dawn of a new age of democracy, equal rights and social justice."[6] Yet, despite efforts to integrate Jews into a modern and secular Polish society by liberals and socialists and by organizations such as the Jewish Labor Bund, anti-Semites wanted Jews eliminated from Poland's economic and social life; they even wanted the issue of Jewish citizenship revisited (Bauer, 2001, p. 151). "For a large percentage of the three million Jews who lived in Poland," which had the largest Jewish population in the world, "the interwar period was one of widespread virulent anti-Semitism, systematic economic discrimination, and increasing violence" (Here and Now, 2002, p. 1).[7]

Many Polish Jews—such as Lusia's father, who owned a fabric store, and Bronka's father, who had a grocery—were shopkeepers. In some skilled occupations such as tailoring and shoemaking, Jews made up the majority; others worked in businesses and the professions, particularly law, medicine, and journalism. And Jews were disproportionately represented among wealthy industrialists. Yet as early as the 1920s the government, by far the largest employer in Poland—more than half a million Jews worked for the government in adminstrative jobs or in factories—had already begun to dismiss Jews (Here and Now, 2002, p. 3). Jewish doctors were no longer employed in state hospitals, and Jewish lawyers couldn't practice in state institutions. Railroad companies dismissed Jewish workers. Shop owners lost their licenses to sell cigarettes and tobacco. By the 1930s, with the further intensification of anti-Semitism, the Polish government ordered that all shops include the name of the owner on their business signs, effectively identifying Jewish-owned businesses in order to facilitate boycotts (Here and Now, 2002, p. 4).

Following the lead of the Nazi party in Germany, the Polish government supported measures adopted by Polish professional organizations to exclude Jews. More than half of the Polish doctors were Jews, yet the inevitable effect of barring them from practicing didn't prevent the Polish Medical Association, in 1937, from incorporating a paragraph into its charter that excluded Jews from the medical profession. The Polish Bar Association endorsed a similar measure, which the government sanctioned. It restricted Jews—who made up one-third of Polish lawyers in addition to other legal professionals—from practicing (Antisemitism, n.d. n.p.).

Subsequent laws, restrictions, and prohibitions affected almost every aspect of Jewish life in Poland. By 1938 "'ghetto benches' in the universities, which segregated Jewish students in separate seats at the back of the class" were implemented (Bauer, 2001, p. 151.) In addition to economic discrimination and the subsequent impoverishment of large numbers of Jews, violence escalated. In 1936, pogroms took place in the town of Przytyk and in other communities. Anti-Jewish demonstrations in Warsaw left many injured and much property destroyed. "During this period, no fewer than 1,289 Jews were wounded in attacks in over 150 towns and villages in Poland. In August of 1937 alone there were four hundred attacks on Jews in seventy-nine cities and towns" (Here and Now, 2002, p. 4).

The situation became progressively more dire in 1939 and 1940, after the German occupation. When the Nazis took over the Jewish factories in Lodz, Jews were forced to do hard, slave labor. Soon, as restrictions tightened almost day by day, the Jewish community was totally unable to function: There was a ban on trade with Jews, all Jewish-owned shops and factories had to be so designated, there was even a ban on walking along the main thoroughfare, Piotrkowska Street, or in municipal parks, and "a requirement to step off the pavement for Germans" (Here and Now, 2002, p. 7). To be easily identifiable, an order was issued for Jews, regardless of age, to wear armbands, "precisely 10 cm. wide and worn on the right arm, just below the armpit" (Here and Now, 2002, p. 12). Later, all Jews were required to wear Stars of David on both the front and back of their garments; failure to follow this order was punishable by death. Beatings and humiliations became more and more frequent. And then—the most grievous wound—the synagogues were set on fire.

The next step would be to segregate and isolate the Jews in their own quarter of the city. Only a month after the German occupation, in October 1939, the first Polish ghetto had been established in Poland, in Piotrkow Tribunalski, a town in Lodz province. However, the first ghetto in a major city was in Lodz. It was both the first to be established—a model for others soon to come—and the last to be liquidated.

Sixty-five years later, the effects of World War II still dominate the Polish landscape: the remains of ghettos, monuments, battle sites, memorials, museums, and, of course, the camps—slave labor camps, internment and concentration camps, death camps. If you look at a map of Poland since the Nazi takeover in 1939, you see that it is spotted with camps, like some kind of disfiguring disease. Today, Poles are offended by the use of the term "Polish concentration camps" and remind you that they were "Nazi camps on Polish soil." They also remind you that they endured huge casualties in the war—about three million non-Jewish Poles died as a result of mass killings, deportations, and imprisonment (which is, coincidentally, the same number of victims as Polish Jews). Poles were second only to Jews in the contempt in which they were held by the Nazis—or perhaps third in line behind the Roma, more commonly known as Gypsies. Browning says that Poland was "destined to become a 'laboratory' for Nazi experiments in racial imperialism, an area where they tried to turn into reality ideological slogans such as *Lebensraum* (living space), *Volkstumskampf* (ethnic or racial struggle), *Flurbereinigung* (a basic or comprehensive cleansing), and *Endlösung der Judenfrage*" (Browning, 2004, p. 14).

Polish anti-Semitism was not the reason that the ghettos were established or that so many camps were situated in Poland. Historians generally agree that it was due to Poland's central location and easy access to railway lines. Yet Jews have to work hard at being sympathetic to Polish victimization because the history of Polish anti-Semitism gave Nazis ample reason to believe that most Poles would be indifferent to the fate of the Jews in their country—and not a few would be willing accomplices.[8]

While, at the best of times, Jews lived peacefully alongside their Polish, mostly Catholic, neighbors, they were always only tolerated as outsiders. They were never included in what political scientist Helen Fein has termed the "compulsory universe of obligation: that circle of persons toward whom obligations are owed, to whom rules apply, and whose injuries call for expiation by the community" as opposed to those who are "outside the boundaries" (1979, p. 33). When threatened, those within the "circle" would be protected by the social, religious, and political institutions of the nation. The most obvious and striking comparison, often cited, that illustrates Fein's concept is of Polish and Danish attitudes. Danes identified with Jewish Danes *as Danes*; that is, Danes of the Jewish faith. As part of the "universe of obligation," Jews had as much right to be protected against the enemy as their Christian countrymen. On the other hand, Fein makes the compelling argument that the exclusion of Jews from the Polish community facilitated Nazi policy and Jewish victimization. And, in fact, in all of the occupied territories of Europe, Denmark had the least number of victims (proportionally) while the largest number of Holocaust victims were Polish Jews (actually and also proportionally).

Whether or not they were aware of it at the time, the lives of the girls who later found each other at the Girls Club were profoundly affected by their exclusion from the protective circle. With the German occupation, however, their lives were transformed, catastrophically and irrevocably. Eventually they would all find themselves either in ghettos and camps—Auschwitz, Bergen-Belsen, Mauthausen, Ravensbruck—or in hiding. The "lucky ones," such as Renia, would be in exile in the farthest, most remote and desolate reaches of the Soviet Union: Siberia, Kazakhstan, Uzbekistan, or, in Irma's case, living as a refugee in America.

The Germans invaded Poland on September 1, 1939. By September 8, they were triumphantly marching through Lodz. Only a few months later, Lusia, Bronka, and Dorka found themselves living in the ghetto, bewildered and frightened. "We were only children. It was very scary," Lusia said, "we were surrounded by wires. There were soldiers with guns and rifles." Frania, what was left of her family, and many other residents would be relocated to Lodz in 1942 when the ghetto was closed in Pabiance, a small town only seventeen kilometers to the south. The four girls were never to meet in the ghetto, but from this time onward they would live parallel, sometimes intersecting lives. Eventually—transformed from the innocent children they were and transported thousands of miles across the ocean—they would come together at the Girls Club.

Not long after the occupation began, the announcement was made: all Jews in Lodz were to be removed from their homes and relocated to a ghetto. Although the Lodz ghetto is of particular relevance to this story, the conditions that existed there were similar to those occurring all over Poland and elsewhere in Europe: overcrowding; starvation and lack of sanitation leading to diseases such as typhus and typhoid fever; lack of services; periodic *Aktions*—roundups, sporadic killings, massacres, deportations to the camps.

Initially, the ghetto was meant to be a holding pen for Jews who were to be deported from Europe: what Christopher Browning, in his intense analysis of events from 1939 to 1942 leading to the "final solution," describes as a "temporary way station on the road to complete deportations" (Browning, 2004, p. 113). Actually, the first plan for deporting Jews from Poland preceded the German occupation. An idea to relocate Jews to Madagascar, a French colony off the coast of Africa, "fantastical in retrospect," was conceived and later abandoned by Polish and French anti-Semites (Browning, 2004, p. 81).[9] Although the SS revived the idea, they soon saw how impractical such a plan was. An alternative plan was considered as well: for Jews to be "resettled" near the easternmost boundary of Poland, on a reservation in a swampy area east of Lublin and close to the River Bug. But after a great deal of disagreement, the illogic of removing such huge numbers of Jews once again became apparent. The Germans then, reluctantly, decided upon ghettoization. But, Browning says,

> many questions had to be decided: the boundaries of the ghetto, the resettlement of Poles and Germans living there, the shifting of traffic patterns, the plans and materials for sealing and guarding the ghetto, the measures to combat epidemics, preparations for sewage removal and disposal of corpses, and the procurement of provisions for feeding and heating. Only when all these preparations had been made and sufficient manpower was on hand would they order the "sudden" creation of the ghetto. (2004, p. 114)

The announcement of the Lodz ghetto came in early February 1940, along with some details that made it the most isolated of all the ghettos in Poland: the physical boundaries of the area that was to become home to Lusia, Dorka, Bronka, and, later, Frania, were identified; times of entry and exit were set;

and numerous restrictions were issued. The ghetto was to be in the northern part of the city, where many Jews already lived, and to be named after a German World War I hero, Karl von Litzmannstadt. As non-Jews were ordered out of the area, the Nazi propaganda effort tried to persuade them that the "ghettoes were necessary in order to protect them from the Jews" who were said to be "carriers of epidemic illnesses" (Bauer, 2002, p. 160). Jews, on the other hand, were told that living in the ghetto would protect them from "Polish thugs who were becoming more and more emboldened in their attacks" (Browning, 2004, p. 114). Both groups were predisposed to easily accept these claims.

Like all the ghettos, the Lodz ghetto was located in the most derelict and dilapidated part of the city, known for its "underworld characters" (Browning, 2004, p. 114). By March 1940, the girls were living in the impoverished *Baluty* quarter, where many of the old wooden houses had no toilets or even running water. Lusia's family was forced from their home on *Aleja Pierwszego Maja* (Avenue of the First of May), "a very nice street in a middle-class neighborhood," she says. In the ghetto they were "crowded together into one room; there was no gas, no water." Lusia's grandmother was with them, her aunts and their families crowded together nearby. Her father had already left Lodz to look for work in Warsaw. Lusia's mother had been forced out of her teaching job; when her father was required to close his shop, the family was left with no livelihood.

Bronka and her parents shared an apartment with a family of German Jews. Her family's circumstances were more modest than those of Lusia and Dorka, and they had lived in a less affluent neighborhood. Her father eked out a living at his grocery store; her mother "helped out" there. "Because we were so poor," Bronka says, wryfully, "the change in our standard of living wasn't all that much apparent at first, when we moved to the ghetto."

In the midst of the bitterly cold winter of 1940 the girls and their families, along with all of the Jews of Lodz, left their homes for the last time. Photos in a 2004 exhibition, *The Children of the Lodz Ghetto*, show streets filled with "endless crowds headed for the ghetto."[10] Some are dragging sleds through the snowy streets, piled high with whatever they were able to hold on to; others are pulling open wagons; many are simply carrying packs on their backs; one young man is carrying a heavy wrought iron headboard on his shoulders. In a memoir, excerpts of which accompanied photos in the exhibition, a witness wrote:

> Frost-bitten and often snow-blinded, long columns of Jews of different social status arduously thronged in the direction of the ghetto—men and women, the old and the children. . . . fighting their way through snow in interminable human serpents, their backs bent by the burden of huge bundles either carried on their shoulders or piled on primitive carts. Some pulled sledges loaded with tables and chairs, kitchen pots and bedding. The bigger stuff . . . had to be left behind." (Podolska, 2004a, n.p.)

When the ghetto was announced, many Jews fled to the countryside. It's doubtful, however, that escape improved their fates. As the surrounding towns and villages were later emptied of Jews, many ended up in the ghetto anyway or were sent directly to the death camps. Like Lusia's father, who left Lodz before the family was relocated to the ghetto, they never returned to their families. Lusia learned of her father's fate years later from friends of the family in Israel. Early in the war, he was deported from the Warsaw ghetto to one of the death camps, most likely Treblinka.

In April 1940, the Lodz ghetto was sealed, "fenced with barbed wire and exits were guarded by police" whose orders were to "shoot to kill." Lodz was "the most completely isolated" of the ghettos. "There was literally no contact with the outside world" (Bauer, 2002, p. 169).

Initially, despite the overcrowding, life in the ghetto was bearable; in Lodz, as in the larger ghettos of Warsaw and Vilna, the inhabitants organized "a rich cultural life during the early period of Nazi occupation" (Dwork, 1991, pp. 187, 188). There were lectures, concerts, children's clubs and youth groups, theatrical presentations, and libraries. Lusia remembers: "The adults tried to give some semblance of normalcy, to give structure." In addition, in keeping with Jewish cultural traditions, social welfare and cultural organizations were established. Not only did they organize much-needed soup kitchens for the poorest of the poor, but they developed procedures to use during epidemics (Tec, 2003, p. 43).

Although Jewish religious practices were forbidden, observant Jews continued to pray, albeit clandestinely and under difficult conditions. Keeping the Sabbath—most had to work—and following the dietary laws were almost impossible. Pregnant women were explicitly permitted to eat non-Kosher meat. And while they were for all practical purposes fasting on most days as a result of meager food allocations, many Jews made a point of fasting on *Yom Kippur*, the Day of Atonement, which is the highest of the Holy Days in the Jewish calendar (Bauer, 2002, p. 192).

Curiously, schools were permitted in Lodz. During 1940 and 1941, the girls were among "14,000 children who attended 2 kindergartens, 34 secular and 6 religious schools, 2 high schools, 2 college-level schools and 1 trade school (weaving)" (Bauer, 2002, p. 194). Bronka remembers attending school in the ghetto for one or two years, studying Yiddish, Hebrew, and German, among other subjects such as instruction in knitting. There even was a summer camp and other facilities used throughout the year in Marysin, a Lodz suburb; Lusia's mother taught school at an orphanage there.

But it wasn't to last. When 20,000 Jews who had been deported from Western Europe arrived in the ghetto, living space became ever more impossible to manage. Schools that were closed in order to house the new arrivals were supposed to reopen and resume classes, but they never did. After that time, Lusia says, "the adults," including her mother and her Aunt Zosia who, before the war, had taught at a *Beys Yaakov*,[11] a religious school for girls, "improvised a simple schooling system, and kept it secret." But when the Germans "had to face up to the unwelcome reality that the ghetto was not going to disappear quickly" (Browning, 2004, p. 116), they made other plans for the children: for the older ones who could be exploited as laborers, and for those who were too young to be useful yet had to be fed and cared for, and simply represented a burden.

The Germans hadn't made long-term plans for the ghetto; they hadn't even made adequate preparations for provisions for the relatively short term. They believed they didn't have to, since their idea was to force the Jews to disgorge their "hoarded wealth" in exchange for food (Browning, 2004, p. 116). Even when starvation became widespread, some persistently held on to the absurd notion that Jews would rather starve than give up their possessions. But as early as August 1940, Browning writes: "The impoverishment of the Jews had increased considerably.... Fully 70% of the population had no means to buy food and were dependent upon the community. By the end of August, however, food deliveries into the ghetto had stopped because the community itself had no more money to purchase the supplies of food already available in the German stockpile" (Browing, 2004, p. 118).

In 1940, the daily food ration in the ghetto was 1,800 calories. By mid-1942 it was 600 calories (Podolska, 2004a, n.p.). In Poland, as a whole, it has been estimated that 20 percent of the ghetto populations died of starvation (Tec, 2003, p. 40).

Deborah Dwork's book, *Children with a Star*, deals with the experiences of children and youth in the Holocaust. She makes it poignantly clear that while children, including the girls of this story, "participated in activities of a former world of childhood, games, groups, clubs, and classes, they were plagued by the rampant and deadly hunger, cold and disease of the ghetto world" (1991, p. 196).[12] Bronka says that her prevailing memory of life during the war was "constant, relentless hunger."

Miraculously, the girls—Lusia, Bronka, Dorka, and Frania—were not among those who succumbed. But child mortality in the Lodz ghetto, primarily from starvation, in just the one brief period from January to August 1941, went from 3 percent to more than 20 percent (Bauer, 2002, p. 185).

Yet children played—because play is their way of making sense of the adult world. Lusia agrees: "We were hungry all the time." But, she points out, "we were still caught up in living every minute. As children we didn't realize what we were going through. Even though there were soldiers with guns, we had to go out, we were only human, we were children." Unfortunately, in the ghetto children "played what they needed to understand, and what they did understand was the horror of an adult world gone mad" (Kestenberg & Brenner, 1996, p. 135).

Death became so commonplace that children would play death games. "They would dig a pit [and] put a child inside" (Levin, 1993, p. 249). They played at picking up the dead who had fallen in the streets and putting them on carts to be removed to the cemeteries. And they learned to ignore the dead lying on the streets, even children. One such incident was witnessed by a Lodz pediatrician "when three boys were playing a game of horses and drivers next to the prostrate body of a dead or dying child." At first the children "ignored" the dead child, but soon became frustrated when "their reins got entangled in him" (quoted in Stargardt, 2006, p. 177): "They try every which way to disentangle them, they grow impatient, stumble over the boy lying on the ground. Finally one of them says: 'Let's move on, he gets in the way.'"

Other games were almost as grotesque as the burials. Children reenacted "executions on the town square. . . . they were also observed acting out Gestapo interrogations, slapping each other's faces" (Stargardt, 2006, p. 114). They played the role of the Germans, who were depicted as powerful, while the Jews—sometimes their own parents—were portrayed as completely submissive. "They enacted scenes of German brutality, such as raids on the ghettos, forced removal of people from their hiding places, massacres, and marches toward the deportation trains" (Levin, 1993, p. 249).

In addition to hunger and starvation, disease and epidemics became a self-fulfilling prophesy: "the ghettos created them," noted Holocaust scholar Yehuda Bauer says (2002, p. 160). Bronka's father was among the thousands who died of typhus in the ghetto. Death, however, could also come from a variety of other sources: from *Aktions*, sporadic killings, and "less directly from forced removals" to Chelmno and elsewhere (Tec, 2003, p. 39).

In 1941, one of the first extermination camps, and the first in which mass executions were carried out by gassing, was constructed in Chelmno, a small village of about 250 people. It was conveniently located for deportations from the Lodz ghetto: The main railway line from Lodz to Poznan ran through the village and was connected to Lodz—which was relatively near, about 55 kilometers—by a branch line. The Chelmno camp was established to exterminate the Jews from the Warthegau, the part of Poland that consisted of the province of Poznania, almost the whole province of Lodz, and a part of the province of Warsaw: 320,000 people were put to death there.[13]

Once the site for the death camp was selected, some buildings were confiscated by the German occupation authorities, and the camp was built in the middle of the town. The first of the transports arrived on December 7 with ghetto inhabitants from the cities and towns of the Warthegau. The extermination process began the following day. Fifty to seventy people at a time were crammed and locked into vans which, on the outside, looked like furniture delivery vans. Then the driver closed the doors and turned on the motor. It took ten excruciating minutes for the victims to suffocate from the gas.

Although Chelmno was constructed for the extermination of Jews, the first to perish there were Roma, or Gypsies. About five thousand Roma were brought to Lodz from Austria at the beginning of November 1941 and were segregated from the Jews in a separate section of the ghetto, the *Zigeunerlager*. Only a few months later, in early January 1942, when a typhus epidemic erupted there, more than four thousand were taken to Chelmo to be gassed.

Chaim Rumkowski, the head of the Lodz Council of Elders, or *Judenrat*, was a very controversial figure. Some have characterized him as a saint and others, Bauer for example, as a ruthless megalomaniac. Rumkowski's strategy was to remain inconspicuous, obey orders, and refrain from anti-Nazi activities. Some of the orders he forced the residents of the ghetto to obey were harsh by any standard. He is, nevertheless, undisputedly credited for having been the one to come up with the scheme for turning the ghetto into a vast factory system: "In early April 1940, shortly before the ghetto was sealed . . . Rumkowski proposed organizing ghetto labor into factories to produce goods for the German war effort . . . in order to purchase food. The Lodz mayor, Dr. Karl Marder, gave him permission to impose a system of forced labor. Marder agreed because he knew there were not enough funds allocated to continue purchasing food" (Browning, 2004, pp. 116, 117).

Despite many internal debates within the Lodz and regional administrations—disagreement came from those who thought providing an alternative means to purchase food would undermine the effort to get Jews to part with their valuables—the Nazi ghetto manager prevailed in his determination to make the ghetto pay for itself. The Lodz ghetto became a mini-factory town; in this respect it mirrored the industrial history of the city. And, in fact, because of its relatively high degree of productivity, the Lodz ghetto, the first to be established, was the last to be liquidated.

Of course there was extreme economic exploitation; workers were able to keep only 35 percent of their meager wages. Yet the ghetto survived; it changed, as Rumkowski intended, from a "temporary device for extracting Jewish wealth before deportation" to "a more permanent institution in whose economic productivity the Germans had a vested interest" (Browning, 2004, p. 119). When the schools were closed, Bronka became one of the ghetto's child laborers: "I worked in a straw factory. The straw was used to make overshoes for the soldiers," she said. Worn over boots, they were used as insulation. "I was paid in money from Germany for working in the factory. But I worked in the dark, and in the freezing cold." Such factories continued to produce clothes and other articles that the German war economy needed until July 1944, when the Soviet army, advancing rapidly through Poland, stopped only sixty miles from Lodz.

Deportation of Jews to Chelmno had begun in mid-January 1942. As the exploitative economic system faced continuing difficulty in sustaining the

ghetto, pressure accelerated to winnow the population of the dependent elderly, ill, and crippled as well as young children. At the end of August 1942,
after the "final solution" was conceived at the notorious Wannsee Conference,
the Germans demanded that thirteen thousand elderly inmates and eight
thousand children, aged ten and under, must be delivered for deportation in
exchange for saving the remaining 80 percent of the ghetto population. It fell
to Chaim Rumkowski to carry out the order: a man, "who felt particularly
close to children, was compelled to ask his fellow Jews to sacrifice the very
young and the old so that the rest could live" (Tec, 2003, p. 69). Here is an account of that time, from *Children of the Lodz Ghetto* (Podolska, 2004a, n.p.):

> September 1, 1942: The first day of another (the fourth) year of the war began
> with horrifying news which reached us early in the morning. The Germans have
> emptied all of the hospitals in the ghetto. From the early morning, hospitals
> have been surrounded by troops and all the patients, no exception made, loaded
> on lorries and taken away from the ghetto. Great panic arose all over the city.
> People finally realized they were doomed.
>   Sept. 4: There was panic. Everyone was trying to get work allocations for chil-
> dren but to no avail. Although there was an effort to register children between
> the ages of 8–10, an announcement came that all of those lists were void.

Deportations to Chelmno averaged one thousand a day, with brief respites,
until March 1943. Among these victims was Lusia's beloved grandmother,
who was taken during one of the deportations of the elderly. Life—such as
it was—for those remaining continued for another terrible year: "constant
hunger, losing everybody, epidemics, deportations" are Bronka's principal
memories of those years.

In April 1944, in connection with the planned liquidation of the Lodz
ghetto, the Nazis decided to renew their extermination activities in Chelmno.
On June 23, 1944, transports to Chelmno from the Lodz ghetto began anew;
7,176 persons had been killed by mid-July. Following the deportations, only
those able to work remained in the ghetto until its liquidation, which was
successfully completed between August 9 and 29 when the remaining 70,000
Jews, except for a small number left behind to work for the Nazis, were sent
to Auschwitz-Birkenau.

Among them were four girls: Bronka, Lusia, Dorka, and Frania.

NOTES

1. Online course offered by the London School of Economics and Political Science, Session 2, given by Anita Prazmowska.

2. There are 386 documents that survived the war in the collection of autobiographies at YIVO. See Moseley; also, Schandler.

3. The Kaminska Theater operates in Warsaw today, alternating performances in Yiddish and Polish.

4. Now Vilnius, in Lithuania.

5. First and second generation Jewish-Americans who grew up in immigrant communities, such as my neighborhood of Brownsville, Brooklyn, will recall similar language patterns. See discussion in Ford, *The Girls*.

6. In Here and Now, YIVO Library, New York, October 28, 2002.

7. An important resource for information on Poland in the interwar years is *Polin: Studies in Polish Jewry*, Volume 8 (1994, September). Jews in Independent Poland, 1918–1939, edited by Antony Polonsky, Ezra Mendelsohn, and Jerzy Tomaszewsk. It is a volume of scholarly papers under the general editorship of Professor Antony Polonsky of Brandeis University, part of a 21-volume series which has been published since 1986. Since 1994 the series has been published by the Littman Library of Jewish Civilization. In March 2000 the series was honored with a National Jewish Book Award by the Jewish Book Council in the United States.

8. There are innumerable writings of Polish–Jewish relations with wide-ranging points of view regarding Polish culpability in Jewish victimization. Bartowszewski, a social anthropologist in Polish-Jewish studies who has been a lecturer at several prestigious universities in England and the United States, rejects this idea as simplistic. For one interesting analysis of Polish-Jewish relations see Zimmerman.

9. Also see Browning's earlier work, *Path to Genocide*, p. 127.

10. The exhibition was held in Lodz in 2004 on the sixtieth anniversary of the liquidation of the ghetto. The accompanying booklet is not paginated.

11. One of the spelling variations. The *Beys Yaakov* or *Beis Yakov* movement was started by seamstress Sarah Schenirer in 1917 in Krakow. While boys attended religious schools, at least in preparation for their *Bar Mitzvot*, there was no formalized system of Jewish education for girls and young Jewish women. Schenirer

started a school of her own, trained other women to teach, and set up similar schools in other cities throughout Europe.

12. Dwork is a professor of history at Clark University and director of the Strassler Family Center for Holocaust and Genocide Studies.

13. According to data from the Central Commision for Investigation of German Crimes in Poland. Also in Browning (2004).

Growing Up

Coming of Age in a Nightmare

When I look back, it's just a bad dream.

—*Betty (Basia Pasternak) Ratchik*

One and a half million children were murdered during the Holocaust; the young women who came to live at the Girls Club were among the small percentage who miraculously survived.[1] Until recently however, child survivors' stories such as theirs, writes Deborah Dwork in *Children with a Star*, were "conspicuously, glaringly and screamingly absent" from the Holocaust literature (1991, p. 253). That literature has been significantly enriched since the voices of child survivors who were "silent for forty years" have begun to be included in collections of witness testimonies (Dasberg, 2001, p. 4).

Just after the end of World War II, a substantial effort *was* made to collect thousands of hand-written children's testimonies. In 1947 they were published in Europe but, over time, they were forgotten or overlooked (Cohen, 2007, p. 73). The collectors were not especially concerned with the testimonies as historical documents since they believed that facts and information concerning the Holocaust were already known through adult witnesses; children's stories, if they were included, were usually footnotes to adult accounts. These children's stories, it seems, served other purposes: psychological and political. Psychologists intuitively understood that telling their stories could perform a healing function for the children, a conclusion that has been supported in many more recent studies.[2] Politically, the stories of these most innocent victims could be used to advance the Zionist agenda in the postwar period.

Except for this brief postwar effort, child survivors were discouraged from telling their stories by well-intentioned adults who wanted them to forget, or believed the children were lucky to have "had little memory of what happened" (Sternberg & Rosenbloom, 2000, p. 14). In addition, the testimony of those who were children during the Holocaust was not sought out because a child's memory, even under normal circumstances, is thought to be highly unreliable, and memory compromised by trauma even more so. Consequently, in contrast with adult survivors, children's stories "were taboo to historians and other professionals, and the media" until the early 1990s when there was a renewed interest in recording their Holocaust experiences (Sternberg & Rosenbloom, 2000, p. 6). Even so, when historian Nicholas Stargardt began researching *Witnesses of War* (published as recently as 2006) in which he reconstructs children's wartime stories, he confesses that he "wondered whether the experience of children counted as 'real' history" (p. xiv).[3]

Dwork's book was one of the first to examine the experiences of children in the Holocaust. It is a sensitive and scholarly account of those "whose fate was marked by their ill-luck to have been Europeans" at a time when the Nazis were engaged in two wars: the war against the Allies and the parallel war they fought against the Jews. Hitler was determined not only to commit genocide against the Jews but to make the "race" extinct (p. xv). Consequently, those who were the future of the "race"—Jewish children such as the girls whose lives later converged at the Girls Club—were a prime target.

For the Jews, the attempt to eradicate Jewish youth was the most grievous of crimes. Traditionally, but also among secular Jews, children are cherished by Jewish families and communities. There are always individual exceptions, of course, which challenge generalizations. But this deeply embedded value has been tenacious in Jewish culture. As noted earlier, even in prewar Poland and despite the ever-increasing poverty among Jews, life remained relatively normal for many children. They were generally "provided for physically, religiously and educationally" (Sternberg & Rosenbloom, 2000, p. 7). They had their friends, they played, they went to school and studied. And they were, as much as possible, sheltered from anti-Semitism. Under normal circumstances it is likely that the women whose stories are told here would have grown up uneventfully—moving from childhood through their teens and into young adulthood—in familiar surroundings and within the shelter of their families.

However, for these girls and many other Jewish children, "for a protracted period. . . . previous familiar anchors—relatives, possessions, home, daily routines, social etiquette, community—had been stripped away" (Haas, 1996a, p. 100). After 1939—when Bronka, Lusia, Dorka, and Frania were transferred to the ghetto; Irma was sent away to an orphanage in France; Basia was put into hiding; Sonia was sent into the woods; and Renia's mother took her to what she believed was safety on the "Russian side"—their circumstances became anything but normal.

In the ghettos and later in the camps, in hiding, or in exile, they survived varying degrees of massive and long-lasting trauma. They spent their developmentally critical childhood and early adolescent years enduring dislocation and suffering extreme deprivation of even the basic necessities of life: food, shelter, warmth, sleep. Their physical development, emotional and psychological adjustment, and social and intellectual development were brutally jeopardized. The title of the book and film, *Girl, Interrupted*, exactly describes what each of the young women experienced.

Eventually, the girls' lives were completely shattered. And the trauma not only extended throughout the war, it persisted through the early postwar years of displacement which, for some, were "as traumatic as the Holocaust itself, and sometimes more so" (Suedfeld, 2002, p. 5). It is remarkable that they were able to survive and, afterward, to restore any semblance of normalcy to their grievously abused minds and bodies. Still more astonishing is that this small group of women went on to build successful new lives.

Even before historians belatedly took notice, the experiences of child survivors of the Holocaust caught the attention of some in the psychosocial fields. Since the early 1990s the literature in this area has become quite extensive. Child survivors became "a new psychosocial issue, and a focus for clinical attention" (Dasberg, 2001, p. 4) when Judith Herman and others began to study Holocaust survivors in the context of post-traumatic stress.[4] Their conclusions are extremely helpful in understanding not only the complexity of reconstructing child survivors' stories, but also in comprehending what the girls endured—and in appreciating their resilience.

Studying child survivors presented researchers with a number of troublesome issues for several reasons. First, some child survivors are simply unable to retrieve their memories, even with the help of specifically trained clinicians. As one survivor, a child hidden during the war, confessed: "I remember nothing about the time I spent with those people. . . . Not a face, not a voice, not a piece of furniture. As if the time I spent there had been a time out of my life" (A. Stein, 1994, p. 107). Her problem is not uncommon.

Although some struggle to remember anything at all, for others perhaps "an even more vexing problem is the intrusion of fragments of memory— most are emotionally powerful and painful but make no sense." These are "experienced as 'crazy' and never shared with anyone" (Krell, 1993, p. 387). Not only children, but all people "who have survived atrocities often tell their stories in a highly emotional, contradictory, and fragmented manner that undermines their credibility" (Herman, 1992, p. 1). But trauma that occurs in childhood may have been stored through the senses, making these "pre-narrative" memories even more difficult to make sense of:

> Memories are recalled from smell and touch. A mother's scent, a hand held by a father. . . . Normal memory can be described as the action of telling a story. Traumatic memory by contrast is wordless and static. The trauma story . . . is a pre-narrative. It does not develop or progress in time, and it does not reveal the storyteller's feelings or interpretation of events. It is like a series of still snapshots or a silent movie." (Rockman, n.d., p. 3)

As a result, it is not unusual for child survivors to doubt the accuracy of their memories; some are not even sure that what they do remember is what they actually experienced or whether it might have been told to them. Still others who remember refuse to discuss the Holocaust: a challenge to historians and others who are now eager to complete the Holocaust record as the number of survivors steadily diminishes. Survivors may have the need to deny or forget but may be conflicted by the equally compelling need to talk about their experiences:

> [N]ot remembering . . . may mean being deprived of a connection with those who loved and nurtured you, yet to have memories may mean that one is never free of the fear and dread of those terrible times. For example, one child survivor's only vivid memory of his mother is the moment when he is torn from her arms into safety while she is pushed into a train to deportation and

death. He never wants to forget his mother, but always wants to forget the train. (Rockman, n.d., p. 2)

As difficult as these circumstances are, not having the testimony of child survivors—disregarding one of the essential missing pieces of the Holocaust story—seriously diminishes our understanding of the total picture. Even those stories that have been filtered through the fractured lens of a child's eye add yet another important dimension to the still-incomplete account. Child survivors, as Dwork pointed out, are not only a fertile but an absolutely unique resource (1991, p. xlii).

Generally, the literature on child Holocaust survivors does not distinguish between children and adolescents; fifteen-year-olds and younger are usually classified as children. This is unfortunate. While they are linked—what takes place during adolescence is very much dependent upon what occurs in childhood—there are also distinct aspects of development in each period. Nor has much been written in which the specific focus is on how the experiences of boys and girls differed except for the important, if obvious, fact that boys were at greater risk if they tried to pass as Gentiles, due to circumcision. Generalizations can be made that encompass the development and maturation of both boys and girls, but there are also specific gender differences in the areas of physiology and biology; intellect and cognition; language development; social-behavioral growth and interaction; and psychological, emotional, and moral development.[5] The experiences of the women in this history provide an opportunity to focus on some of the specific challenges they faced as they came of age in the nightmare of the Holocaust.

Each girl's physical development was at risk, whether she was in the ghetto, in hiding, or in exile. In the ghettos and elsewhere, lack of sanitation led to conditions in which typhoid fever flourished. Fleas, lice, bedbugs, and vermin led to illness and infections from scratching and scabies. The girls even lacked adequate sleep, the most elemental and essential need for growing children and adolescents. Lack of heating, inadequate clothing for the bitterly cold winters, and lack of ventilation in the hot summers weakened their immune systems, leading to respiratory infections and, in extreme cases, to tuberculosis. After liberation, it took Lusia months to recover from a mild case of tuberculosis that almost prevented her from coming to the United States.

Renia was immediately sent to a hospital upon her arrival in America because of a lesion on her lungs.

But the primary threat to normal physical development was starvation and severe weight loss. As we know today, after having studied young people who starve themselves as a result of anorexia or bulimia, starvation has many negative, long-term effects. These may include stunted growth, the inability to develop strong bones, or bone diseases such as osteopenia or even osteoporosis—conditions generally associated with the elderly (Kestenberg & Brenner, 1996, p. 44). People with severe weight loss may suffer nerve damage and other neurological problems. There may even be structural changes to the brain. Diseases brought about by weakness and susceptibility can cause other enduring problems as well. Often sufferers will have problems related to anemia or gastrointestinal illnesses. While Sonia lived in the forest she had to forage for food; she ate whatever she could find. She tried to eat berries, roots, anything that could be digested. One time she found some wild wheat and chewed on the raw grain. The diet ultimately had severe effects on her digestive system that plagued her all her life.

When a girl's physical development from childhood to adolescence follows its normal course, she becomes preoccupied with her changing body. Her menstrual periods begin, her hips become rounder, and she sees the first budding of her breasts which, over the next few years, develop into a womanly weight and shape. But not one of the girls had normal periods during the war. All suffered from dismenorrhea or amenorrhea; Bronka got her period only once, on the day she arrived in Auschwitz. Then she didn't menstruate again until after the war, when she was seventeen. Lusia had her period twice, both times in the ghetto:

> My mother didn't tell me much before it came; I spoke with friends about it. Then it left me for about a year and a half: there was no food. I was skin and bones. I just had two eyes.
>
> One day, I hemorrhaged in the street when I was going over a bridge. I was very young; I didn't want people to see me, I was embarrassed. Or maybe scared. I knew it was my period coming back. After that time I don't think I got it again until way after the war.

Dwork writes that amenorrhea was so common that many young women she interviewed were convinced that the Germans "added a chemical to their food to prevent them from menstruating" (Dwork, 1991, p. xxxvi). They believed that the Germans, in their effort to annihilate the Jewish people, would have tried to prevent women from having children. "Even if the Germans were to lose the war, the women said, and even if each individual . . . survived, the poison she had eaten would prevent her from ever conceiving children; thus the Jewish people would die out sooner or later" (Dwork, 1991, p. xxxvi). Many continued to be convinced even when presented with evidence to the contrary.

The consequences of amenorrhea can't be overstated. If they didn't menstruate, girls would not mature. In the ghettos, if they looked young or especially frail, they were in greater jeopardy of being sent away to the camps, where children were usually taken directly to the gas chambers. Dorka remembered how worried she was. "Because," she said, "I looked too young. I was fourteen but I was too small, I was underdeveloped like a child. I didn't even have breasts yet." Thus, a circumstance over which they had no control could determine their fate. Lusia says: "The Nazis let me live because I looked a little older, I started to develop. That saved me. I was the right age." After the war it took months, or even years, to recover from the consequences of such extreme and sustained malnutrition and weight loss.

If a girl's psychological and social development is normal, by the time she is a teenager she is preoccupied with herself, thinking that she is the center of attention. She tries out different personalities, different attitudes, different beliefs.[6] She tests the boundaries of her independence. But such issues need to be worked through in a social context that includes family and peers. Unlike those in hiding, who were completely isolated from others, in the early days of the ghettos children and teenagers did have opportunities to interact with their families and to socialize with young people of both sexes. In the larger ghettos such as Warsaw, Lodz, and Vilna children's clubs and youth groups were organized.

Among teens, an inevitable part of socializing is testing out sexual relationships—they experience their first kisses, the first awkward, groping, sexual experimentation. Then they share their secrets with their friends—sharing information as well as misinformation. Gradually, as they become older, their relationships become more serious and intimate. However, in situations of extreme peril, with death a constant threat, it's not difficult to understand why teenagers would want to experience everything that was possible within their extremely limited circumstances. As a result, Lusia remembers, there was "a lot of sexual experimentation, even promiscuity." She says: "I had no boyfriends then. Many friends did; most girls slept around. One girl said to me: 'I don't want it to grow rusty.' But I was very careful, that's how I was brought up. I wouldn't feel clean. Maybe I was scared I didn't know enough, or maybe I was afraid to become pregnant." Ironically, because starvation prevented most girls from menstruating, pregnancy was not likely—sparing potential young mothers and their babies from certain death.

In addition to learning how to negotiate social relationships, young people in the Holocaust faced challenges related to their intellectual development. Following a normal course, as they become teenagers, young people begin to think in a different way: to imagine what could be, to intellectually assess possibilities. They not only learn about the world, they may imagine an ideal world and, with adolescent optimism, may believe they can help it come to pass. Closely connected to intellectual development is moral development; young people begin to have a more sophisticated sense of right and wrong, to sort through options and choices and to define their own value systems.[7] These changes, "learning to think in a new key," as the noted child psychologist David Elkind calls it, occur with intellectual maturation, and it is in school that these new abilities can be practiced (1998, p. 25).

As noted in the previous chapter, the girls who lived in Lodz were able to continue with their formal schooling in the ghetto for a while. After the schools were closed, only Lusia remembers having what she referred to as "improvised" schooling, provided by her mother and aunt, who had been teachers before the war. Sometimes children had their older siblings' books or lessons, so they could progress somewhat in their learning. However, as conditions worsened, Lodz ghetto youth became preoccupied with survival, neither socializing nor learning. Children in hiding were, of course, totally deprived of schooling during most or all of the war years. Each girl had at least a five-year gap in her schooling.

Overall, healthy child development requires a secure and stable environment. Because children and adolescents are relatively powerless in comparison with adults, they depend upon their parents to love and care for them, to provide shelter, nourishment "and a predictable life" (Sternberg & Rosenbloom, 2000, p. 14), circumstances necessary for healthy development to take place. Judith Herman says that in the absence of these conditions—and, in fact, in the presence of their opposites—the possibility of developmental problems is greatly increased, particularly with regard to what she refers to as the "formation of identity, the gradual separation from the family of origin and the exploration of a wide social world" (1992, p. 61).

Most of the girls retained a sense of security in the initial years of the war, since their families remained relatively intact. Even under the circumstances of life in the ghettos, not having had an early separation from at least one parent may have helped them endure what was to come and provided them with an important base for their later psychological adjustment. Some children, however, rather than feeling secure, learned to mistrust the parents upon whom their care depended (although this feeling was never expressed by the women of the Girls Club, who invariably idealized their parents). Some became contemptuous of adults, including their parents, for being as powerless as they were to change their circumstances. They saw their parents becoming overwhelmed when they were unable to resist or to escape, when there was no action they could take to defend themselves and their families (Herman, 1992, p. 4). They saw basic principles of morality violated by their parents who, in desperation, would lie or cheat or steal—some even stole their children's share of their meager food rations. Their role models, of prime importance in their moral development, increasingly failed to live up to acceptable criteria.

In addition to losing morally principled role models, the children saw traditional gender roles become confused. For men, "the ghetto created a more definite rupture between their prewar and wartime roles . . . their slavelike ghetto existence meant that most men experienced ghetto life as a constant reminder of their failure to live up to their traditional masculine roles," wrote Nechama Tec (2003, p. 53), particularly the roles of provider and protector. For a time, "women's roles retained a semblance of continuity, for their ghetto activities allowed them to fulfill their traditional nurturing roles" (Tec, p. 53). But as men were deported to labor camps or to death camps, many women had to take on the role of head of household. In Lodz, for example, "ghetto conditions forced women to find work when having a job became a prerequisite for survival. From 1942 on, anyone who was not working was regarded as superfluous and was deported. By 1944, when the final census was taken in the Lodz ghetto, virtually all the women were working (and 60% of all workers were women)" (Ofer & Weitzman, 1998, p. 9).

Consequently, there was no aspect of the girls' development in childhood and adolescence —intellectual, psychological, social, moral, physical—that was not adversely affected for at least some period of time by circumstances, conditions, and events which were "impossible" for those who didn't experience them "to imagine," as one child survivor very gently told me. She was not being dismissive; she was simply stating a fact.

In the ghettos, children and teens witnessed unfathomable cruelty, to which the games described in the previous chapter attest. Far too many were bewildered by the sudden disappearance of their parents; those who were fortunate were left with surviving family members. They suffered illnesses, diseases, and constant hunger. As they grew older they were forced to work long hours, in intolerable conditions. Yet, as difficult as their lives had become, they were still with their families: ever-diminishing, to be sure, but they were not yet entirely without family—not yet. It is *in this context only*, during the long years Lusia, Bronka, Dorka, and Frania spent in the Lodz ghetto, that they had a closer semblance to normalcy than the girls who were in hiding and who suffered different types of deprivation and trauma.

While each child's experience was unique, in hiding they shared some basic, common elements. "The first of these was a fundamental lack of comprehension . . . of why they were forced to leave their homes, their families, their friends" (Dwork, 1991, p. 69). How could children possibly understand what was beyond the comprehension of the most informed adults?

Children were generally hidden in two basic ways: formally, through an organization such as Zegota, the Council of Aid to Jews, which was sanctioned by the Polish government in exile and received "small amounts of funding via the underground"; or OSE, the Ouvre de Secours aux Enfants (Nicholas, 2005, p. 372).[8] Informally, and for a variety of reasons, an impromptu decision would be made to send children away to be physically hidden in an abandoned farmhouse or building, or they were told to run off into the forest where they might join with groups of roaming children or adults, or attach themselves to a partisan group. Some children whose parents were killed escaped into hiding on their own.

Others were sent off to be hidden by courageous Gentiles, sometimes friends, if such arrangements could be made—much to their own peril and that of those caught harboring a Jew. Basia was hidden in the cellar of her family's former housekeeper; it was to one of the OSE homes in France that Irma was sent; and Sonia, when her mother learned of an imminent liquidation of the ghetto, was sent off into the woods.

Can there be anything more difficult for parents than to acknowledge that the only way to save their children was to send them away? Such sacrifice and such torment is what Basia, Sonia, and Irma's parents had to bear. As Dwork wrote:

> [F]irst and foremost the children were saved by their parents. The act of giving up one's child, of surrendering one's own daughter or son, of recognizing that one no longer could protect and shelter that small person to whom one had given life, was the first and most radical step in the chain of rescue. It was a paradox: to save one's child one had to accept that one was unable to protect and defend the child. Whether one relinquished that son or daughter to a stranger, a resister, that initial act of abdication was the fundamental beginning. (1991, p. 65)

Once they were in hiding, most children lost all contact with the outside world; they had no opportunities for learning, either formally or informally; they were not able to interact socially either with other children or adults. They were completely vulnerable, without adults they could trust to care for them. Most children and teenagers had no idea of what had happened to their families or friends—whether they were still alive. They may have been, literally, in the dark—that is, hidden in dark places for days or months at a time. They didn't know whether they would have food and water enough to survive or how long they would have to remain hidden (Kustanowitz, 1999, p. 10). They were isolated, disoriented, afraid, "decontextualized and lonely. . . . without mobility or access to either goods or services (food, clothes, shoes, medicines, books, medical care, dentistry)," writes Dwork (1991, p. 68).

Until recently—like adults in hiding or Jews who were exiled to the Soviet Union—hidden children were not considered true Holocaust survivors.[9] As they themselves readily acknowledge, they did not experience the horrors of the ghettos or worse, the shock, terror, and misery of the slave labor and death camps. Among the women of the Girls Club, those who went into hiding did not think of themselves as true survivors; they considered themselves the lucky ones among the group, even though they, like other hidden children, "lost family, friends, and a way of life, and all paid a steep psychological price in order to survive" (Kustanowitz, 1999, p. 12). Basia says: "Compared to the others, I was on a vacation."

Basia's "vacation":
The details are vague, and Basia doesn't care to discuss more than the bare facts—"when I look back," she says, "it's just a bad dream." And she was very young, the youngest of the group, only seven when the war started. But it is possible to fill in some of the blanks from the historical record and from the diary that was kept by her brother, Janek (Pasternak, n.d., n.p.).

Basia was born in 1932, in Tarnopol (Ternopil), in Eastern Galicia, not far from the Ukrainian border. Place names in this part of Polish Ukraine are in multiple languages since, at various times in its history, the region had been incorporated into Poland, the Russian or the Austro-Hungarian Empires, and the Soviet Union. The city is now in Ukraine. In 1939, Tarnopol was part of Poland, a sizable city of forty thousand; 50 percent of the population was Polish, 40 percent Jewish, and 10 percent Ukrainian.[10]

Although the early 1930s were a difficult time for Jews in Poland—in the midst of the worldwide depression, the government instituted major economic restrictions against the Jews—Basia's father had a still-functioning textile store. Basia believes the Pasternak family of five—she had an older brother and sister—lived a normal life. But normality came to an end for seven-year-old Basia and her family when, due to the German-Soviet pact, the Red Army occupied eastern Poland. The troops entered Tarnopol on September 17, 1939, barely two weeks after the Germans invaded Poland from the west.

One of the first things the Soviets did was to set up "special committees" to nationalize property; Jews were their first targets. Consequently, many Jewish businessmen, shopkeepers, factory owners, and artisans lost their livelihoods. And to make matters worse, they were unable to get work permits, since they had been placed in a special category of "inimical elements" or "non-productives." The committees also went through Jewish homes and apartments, confiscated furniture and other private belongings and, often, the apartments as well. When their homes were taken over for the use of Soviet officials, their occupants were forced to find lodging elsewhere in Tarnopol or outside the city.

The Jews' situation continued to deteriorate until July 1941, when the Soviet-German war broke out and the Germans occupied Tarnopol—then it got worse. The city's Jewish population, which had grown in the early phase of the war as Jews from other parts of Poland sought refuge in the Soviet-occupied territories, was immediately subjected to Nazi brutality. Only two days after the Nazis entered Tarnopol, a pogrom began; it lasted from July 4 to July 11. The Nazis, joined by Ukrainian police, took Jewish men out of their homes and shot them in the courtyards. Jews were kidnapped in the streets and taken to collection points, where they were also shot and killed. One of the synagogues was the site of mass murder when it was burned down, along with all the Jews who were inside. During the week of the pogroms, it has been estimated that five thousand Jews were killed in the city and in the surrounding forests and countryside.

A couple of months later, during the High Holy Days of September 1941, the order came to establish a ghetto for Tarnopol Jews and others who had come into the city from nearby *shtetls* and villages. Conditions in the ghetto soon were almost identical to those described earlier in Lodz; it was located in a very poor and neglected neighborhood, mostly without sewers and only a few wells. There were relatively few houses, all in very poor condition. The area, which had had a population of four to five thousand, exploded to at least twelve to thirteen thousand. Some families shared a single room, some lived in attics or in cellars, and some in the synagogues.

By 1942, deportations to the death camps, Belzec and Treblinka, had already begun. According to Basia's brother Janek's diary, on August 31, 1942, their parents were among those who had been assembled in a square, herded onto trucks, and taken to the railroad station where almost two thousand Jews were loaded into freight cars. In the confusion, their parents had already been separated. When they were last seen, Basia's mother was in the third freight car, her father was in the eighth; one can only imagine their despair. But Basia and her sister, Janek learned, had not been deported. They had hidden in the basement of their apartment building, only the first of several hiding places: some were constructed behind false walls, some were dug-out "bunkers" which Basia remembers as nothing more than a "hole in the ground."

Although the ghetto was fenced in, it was not completely isolated as in Lodz. An important consequence of that fact is that Janek, who was working in a labor camp outside the ghetto at that time, was ultimately able to arrange for Basia to go into hiding in the home of a Polish woman, a former worker or maid who was paid to take her in. About ten years old at that time, Basia was placed in some kind of cellar under the house that let in a bit of light and ventilation. Eventually, Basia's brother and sister came into hiding with her.

Once a day, until the town was "liberated" by the Soviet army, the Polish woman brought food and collected the waste. Basia believes the woman regretted her decision after a while. Very likely it became more and more difficult for her to secure food, she could have raised suspicions about why she needed so much, and she undoubtedly worried about the secrecy. But once it was done there was no alternative; they all would have been killed. "The punishment for sheltering Jews, promulgated on October 15, 1941, was death, as was the penalty for leaving the ghettos without permission" (Nicholas, 2005, p. 373).

In June 1943, Basia was among the fewer than two hundred Jews who came out of hiding when the Soviets recaptured the city. It was at that time that she learned that her parents were among the five thousand Jews deported to Belzec in August and September 1942.

Sonia with the partisans:

Unlike Basia, many children had to fend for themselves if they managed to escape when their parents were sent away to the camps or were killed. These children "suffered unbelievably as they wandered around the countryside, orphaned and abandoned, tormented by hunger and freezing weather" (Sternberg & Rosenbloom, 2000, p. 11). Occasionally they succeeded in escaping to the forests and joining partisan groups. Sonia Labiner was one of these children.

The Labiner family lived in the small town of Peremyshlyany, in Galicia, not far from where Basia had lived before the war. The official town website now notes: "The town is Ukrainian speaking and Ukrainians are most of population there. No Jews or Poles left" (Peremyshlyany, n.d., para. 7).[11]

Despite the backwater nature of the town, Sonia's middle-class family was fairly assimilated, not strictly observant, and fluent in both Polish and Yiddish. Sonia was close to her mother, a homemaker, whom she remembered helping with chores, chatting, sharing stories. In 1939, Sonia, her mother, a younger brother, and her baby sister were living with their maternal grandparents. Sonia's father was away, possibly looking for work; Sonia suspected that "looking for work" was a euphemism used by her mother to avoid discussing other reasons her father might not have been at home, in what Sonia thought might have been a troubled marriage. Sonia was very bright and a very good student. When the war broke out, she was studying Russian at a Labor-Zionist school.[12]

After the Nazis occupied the town, sometime in 1941 or 1942, the schools were closed. Soon afterward the family—Sonia's father was back with them by this time—had to move to a ghetto, probably in one of the nearby cities. In 1943 a rumor circulated that there was to be a deportation of children. But when Germans were heard outside the doors arresting Jews, it seemed not only the children but the entire ghetto was being liquidated. Sonia's mother, undoubtedly frantic, sent her out the back door shouting, telling her to "run, run, don't look back." Almost immediately afterward, Sonia's family was murdered.

In a memoir written by Sonia's close friend and confidant, in which he retells some of her story, Seymour Kleinberg wrote: "Her mother saved her by sending her away, by her urgent injunction for her to live. Sonia's boisterous brother was kept by her side; he was too unpredictable, too unreliable to be sent with her. She kept him and he died; she sent Sonia away and she lived" (Kleinberg, 2002, p. 64). Sonia lived—haunted by that knowledge.

Sonia fled into the forest, where many Jews from the town had taken refuge. She wandered about for several days when, unbelievably, she came across two of her relatives—an aunt and cousin—who had found shelter, a hiding place in a farmhouse attic. They shared what they could with her, though they had just about nothing themselves. Yet they were somehow able to sustain themselves. Sonia remembered being desperately hungry, going from campfire to campfire looking for food. On one occasion, when she saw potatoes cooking, she stole one by plunging her hand into the pot of boiling water.

Subsequently, Sonia's aunt made contact with a group of Jewish partisans, underground fighters. Partisans could be found in all of the Nazi-occupied countries, although the exact nature of each group was determined by different conditions and by the group's specific objectives (Tec, 2003, p. 261). There were many variations: they were more, or less, organized; they had a good supply of, or were in need of, weapons; some were primarily engaged in sabotage, others were organized for rescue; they were, or were not, affiliated with armies or governments in exile. Some partisan groups, made up of Soviet soldiers who had fled into the forests, had the support of the Soviet Union. After the Nazi-Soviet pact collapsed in 1941, the Soviet Union had a vested interest in supporting anti-Nazi groups (Tec, 2003, p. 270).

What these partisan groups, ragtag armies, had in common was their "mutual aim to end German oppression" (Tec, 2003, p. 261); they all fought the Nazis. However, in some places such as Poland and parts of the Soviet Union, they also, sadly, fought each other. Jews and non-Jews generally formed separate partisan groups since Jews were as fearful of some Polish resistance groups as they were of being caught by Nazis; some were not only "anti-Nazi but also antisemitic [sic]" (Anflick, 1999, p. 40). Just because the Poles hated the Germans, who were determined to enslave them, did not mean that many Poles hated the Jews any less than they had before the war.

The non-Jewish groups had a decided advantage, since the Jews had neither families nor communities to whom they could appeal for support—food, supplies, or an occasional night of relative comfort in a dry barn. The Polish partisans were courageous: they chose to resist rather than to capitulate or remain neutral and hope for the best, or even collaborate with the Germans. But Jews such as Sonia, her aunt, and her cousin, who had escaped into the precarious shelter of the forests, had no such alternatives—nor had they anything to lose.

Not long after they found the small group of Jewish partisans, Sonia's aunt left her with her cousin—several years her senior. Soon, in a pattern typical for women with partisan groups, Sonia's cousin took a lover, a *tavo*, who became her protector.[13] Tec explains: "Unprotected women were targets, both from men encountered in the countryside and from partisans who expected sexual favors. . . . Often their protection, their very survival, depended on their willingness and ability to form a sexual liaison" (Tec, 2003, pp. 311– 313). Other girls also had lovers, but Sonia was a bit too young and was treated as one of the children. She became "a mascot, nicknamed the *goniff,* the thief" (Kleinberg, 2002, p. 64).

Sonia remained in the forest for eighteen months until, after liberation by the Soviet army, everyone came out of hiding. She was then taken to an orphanage somewhere in the Ukraine. By this time a jaded fifteen-year-old, she never admitted that she was Jewish and, apparently, was fluent enough in Russian to be believable.

Irma, the first to come to America:

Irma Stermer, one of Sonia's close friends at the Girls Club, was the only one of the group who was not Polish. And Irma's story is different from theirs in a number of other ways. She was not from a poor *shtetl* or from a cosmopolitan city. Irma was born and spent her earliest years in a beautiful town, now an upscale lakeside resort, in the Austrian mountains. But the most significant difference is that, although she, too, is a survivor, Irma had not shared their wartime experiences.

Like Basia, Irma believes she was one of the "lucky" ones. She was one of the children—they totaled ten thousand—who were transported from Austria when the *Anschluss*, the annexation of Austria by Germany, occurred. It is true, of course, that in comparison with the Polish girls who lived through the war in the ghettos and the camps, in hiding or in exile, Irma was spared the worst. But she is no less a survivor of the Holocaust. Each person's loss is no less grievous because others may have borne even more sorrow.

Irma sent me a chronology of "significant events" in her life:

—Born November 7, 1929, in Gmunden, Austria.
—March 1938. Hitler invades Austria. Moved out of home to a furnished room with frail mother and baby sister. Father had escaped to Palestine on an illegal transport.
—Spring 1939. Left on a transport for France to live in an OSE children's home.
—June 1940. Hitler invaded France. Children's home had to flee south.
—September 1941. Sent to the United States on another children's transport.

"Of course," Irma realizes, "the Nazis and later the war were the underlying cause for the kind of experiences I had." But she also insists, quite remarkably: "It wasn't really the war that affected my life." When the bare bones of Irma's listing above are fleshed out, however, a life-altering story is revealed.

Gmunden am Traunsee, where Irma was born, is a city that sits on a deep lake surrounded by high mountains. It has a long history: It was founded in the fifth century and by the twelfth century was protected by a circle of walls. Gmunden was important in the early salt trade, became known for its ceramics, and was famous as a spa. Irma's parents were Olga and Simon Stermer. Her mother was a housewife, her father was a combination salesman and deliverer of periodicals for his brother-in-law's publishing firm; Irma had a baby sister, Herta. The family was secular; in fact, there was no synagogue in Gmunden. Irma remembers attending services only on High Holy Days, when the family visited her grandparents in Linz.

Irma doesn't recall experiencing anti-Semitism before the Germans came. "I know my father had many Austrian friends," she says, "and he told stories about how, after Hitler came, his friends who were Austrian country folks would clap him on the back and say to him, 'Ah Stermer, what are you worried about? Just put on a Nazi armband and nobody will bother you.'" As she remembers it: "The only anti-Semitic thing that was ever addressed to me was after Hitler came. I remember some kids calling me Sau-Jud (Jewish pig), and my calling them back Sau-Christ (Christian pig) and proudly telling about this to someone (probably my mother). I was very proud of having done that."

Repressive measures against Jews were instituted soon after the *Anschluss*. The now-familiar story took place: Jews were no longer allowed to work, children were no longer allowed to go to school, and, subsequently, Austrian Jews from Irma's region and elsewhere were ghettoized in Vienna. Before Irma's family was forced to move, "after the *Kristallen Nacht* [sic] on November 10th 1938," she says, "the Germans held a big roundup." The Nazis came to her house to arrest her father, but he was able to evade them and escaped by boarding a train to Linz, where he knew that Viktor, his wife's brother, was in jail. Viktor was able to be released, most likely because at that time it was still possible to get out of jail if you were leaving the country immediately.

Simon, Irma's father, returned home surreptitiously, "packed a rucksack" and left again. With Viktor's help, they "managed to join a transport of men who were going to try to enter Palestine illegally." They did, in fact, get into Palestine by dropping anchor and swimming some distance to the shore. Irma's father couldn't swim, but he was able to float while holding onto Viktor, who pulled him along. The men were met by Jews who had been expecting the transport. Some years after the war, Irma learned from her uncle—she never saw her father again—that the two men joined the British army and fought in North Africa.

Irma says that transports such as the one her father and uncle had taken were "organized for women also, and for children, but neither were able to take babies. So my mother and baby sister and I stayed behind in the one-room furnished apartment in the ghetto, in Vienna." By March 1939, her mother was no longer able to care for Irma and arranged for her to be taken to France where she lived, in succession, in three different children's homes that were managed by the OSE. In the homes, children lost contact with their parents. "The only mail we could get from them was an occasional note of about twenty-five words which the Swiss Red Cross forwarded to us. Many of us," Irma says, "including me, lost track of where our parents were." Yet, she says, she loved living in the OSE homes:

> [On] my very first night in the first children's home . . . the girl in the bed next to me stayed awake with me for a very long time and told me all about life in the home and how everything worked, what I could expect and what would be expected of me. She was the same age I was (nine years old). It's just that she had been there a little longer, and so she told me all about it.
>
> The homes were run in a very democratic way. There was great emphasis on honesty, equality and justice. We even had our own children's court. Misdeeds or trying to get away with something was really looked down upon. There were no warnings, there was no preaching, no know-it-all attitudes. There was a feeling of equality. Everyone lived by the same standards and took them seriously. You were an "insider" just by being there.

The reason Irma lived in three different homes, each one further south, was because the children were forced to flee from the encroaching German army. There was no panic, since the adults didn't let the children know why they were moving. But conditions got progressively more difficult. By the summer of 1941, the OSE began to evacuate the children and arranged to have some of them sent to America. Between June and September 1941, three transports brought about two hundred children from the OSE homes to the United States. They were assisted by the American Friends (Quakers) Service Committee in Marseilles. Irma remembers it well:

> The first step was for all of us to stay at a flea-bitten hotel in Marseille while our papers were put in order. There were some problems with mine and a certificate "in lieu of passport" was made out for me.
>
> In September 1941 we boarded a train which was to take us to Lisbon. We stayed overnight in a convent in Madrid and then continued to Portugal. We

boarded a ship called the Serpa Pinto. And, accompanied by American Quakers, we sailed for America.

The ship, which arrived in Hoboken, New Jersey, on September 24, 1941, was one of the last to bring children here before America entered the war in December. In France, in 1942—a few months after Irma arrived in America—while the OSE organized underground networks, desperately trying to smuggle the children to neutral countries, the police began roundups and deportations from orphanages to Nazi concentration and extermination camps.

Over the previous four years Irma had lost her home, family, and friends. When she was an eight-year-old child, Irma was separated from her father, with whom she was never reunited (although they were in touch with each other after he settled in Israel). Her grandmother perished in Terezin. Irma recently learned (through information she received from Yad Vashem) that her mother and baby sister, Herta, were killed at Maly Trostinec, a concentration camp in Belarus, toward the end of the war.[14] Irma had been sent to live in a foreign country, in children's homes from which she and her protectors were repeatedly forced to flee. She was taken away on a ship, for an ocean voyage of thousands of miles. And then, in a strange new country, Irma was placed in the care of strangers. Like Renia, whose story follows, Irma was clearly one of the "lucky ones."

Renia's story of exile:
Very few Jews of the small town of Sanok survived the war, a few hundred at most, and among them were only a handful of children. Those who did survive, including Renia, were not hidden; they represent an irony of the Holocaust which is not well known.

In 1945, of the 3.3 million Jews who lived in Poland prior to World War II, there were only 300,000 survivors. Of those, approximately 80 percent escaped the Holocaust as a result of Stalin's deportation of Jews to the far-eastern regions of the Soviet Union—to Siberia and to the *stans* of Central Asia: Uzbekistan, Kazakhstan, Turkmenistan, Kyrgyzstan, and Tajikistan. Those who survived the conditions in these harsh, remote, and sometimes desolate regions—huge numbers are said to have perished due to diseases and starvation—also survived the Holocaust.

When Renia's father died of a heart attack in 1934, her mother took Renia (she was four years old at the time) and her older sister from Jaslo to live with their maternal grandparents in the nearby town of Sanok. The San River, which ran through the town, was a demarcation line for the Germans and the Russians in their agreed-upon partition of Poland; at the same time that the Nazis occupied the western side of the city, eastern Sanok fell under Soviet rule.

Shortly before the Soviet occupation, Renia had contracted polio, leaving her left arm semi-paralyzed. For this reason, her mother took her across the river to the "Russian side" first, leaving Renia's grandparents and her sister behind. She left Renia with a Jewish family there, expecting to return as soon as possible. Her mother's plan was to move farther eastward through the Soviet occupied area of Galicia, to Lvov, where Renia's aunt and uncle lived. The town, now in Ukraine, was the third-largest Jewish community in prewar Poland.[15]

Renia, now nine years old, waited for her mother to return for her—but in vain. She received a few postcards from her mother but never saw her again. Somehow, her aunt managed to take her to Lvov. But she was not there very long; in April 1940 she was deported to Siberia, along with hundreds of Lvov Jews and refugees from other towns.

The journey, which may have followed the route of the Trans-Siberian Railroad, was about 2,500 miles. At that time—with primitive conditions, minimal sanitation, and little food—it took a train weeks to cross the vast Russian steppes and reach its destination: in this instance Asino, a city in the Tomsk region of western Siberia which, after 1938, was connected to the Trans-Siberian by a spur. There Renia and her aunt and uncle were incarcerated in a slave labor camp. They were housed with at least one other family in a single room in a former military barracks; they were permitted out on Sundays.

Renia's uncle was put to work as a laborer in the forest, since Asino was an important locus of the lumber industry—until 1941, when Germany invaded the Soviet Union. After the USSR joined the Allies, British and exiled Polish leaders arranged an amnesty for all Poles on Russian territory. When Renia's aunt and uncle were given permission to relocate within the Soviet Union they chose the city of Namangan, in eastern Uzbekistan, about two hundred miles east of Tashkent.

Renia didn't live with her aunt and uncle in Namangan. They rented a small room for themselves and placed Renia in a Polish orphanage, where she was cared for and attended school. As Irma had been, Renia was happy to be with other children and also to visit her aunt and uncle on weekends. In 1945, when the war ended, Renia was fifteen.

Although she did not yet know their fates, by then she had lost her mother, her sister, her grandparents, and most of her family in the great void of the Holocaust. Renia had been in exile for at least five years. Yet, she says, "I was blessed, I didn't suffer so much."[16] Like Irma, Renia had been one of the "lucky" ones. She hadn't lost everything; she hadn't lost her life. And she had been spared the most awful fate of the camps.

As we will see, the girls who had been living in the Lodz ghetto were not to be so fortunate.

NOTES

1. There are no accurate figures; about 10 to 11 percent is the closest estimate. Hiam Dasberg estimates that there were more than 100,000 survivors who were younger than nineteen at the time of liberation; 65,000 of them were under fifteen.

2. See Cohen, Danieli, and others; see also Rosenthal on "The Healing Effects of Storytelling."

3. Stargardt is a fellow of Magdalen College, Oxford, where he teaches modern European history.

4. See Krell, 1993, "Child survivors of the Holocaust: Strategies of adaptation"; J. Marks, 1995, *The Hidden Children: The Secret Survivors of the Holocaust*; I. Modai, 1994, "forgetting childhood," and others. Stargardt resists descriptions that rely on labels such as PTSD (post-traumatic stress disorder), which he believes stereotypes survivors. He cautions against untested assumptions and generalizations that do not fit all situations or individuals. His points are well-taken; it is always necessary to examine where the individual experience intersects with a generalization. However, generalizations are necessary for making broader statements.

5. Drawing upon the classic work of Erik Erikson and others.

6. See the work of David Elkind.

7. For more on moral development, see Carol Gilligan.

8. OSE was an organization which began in Russia, moved to Germany, and then to France where it adopted the French name. Also, see Dwork, p. 38. For more on Zegota, see Dwork, p. 55.

9. In 1991, the first Hidden Child Gathering was held. Subsequently, the Hidden Children Foundation was established to help bring hidden children together, from all over the world, to share their stories (Kustanowitz, 1999, p. 52). A quick Google search reveals a number of other organizations. Irma was recently contacted by one of these groups.

10. Information taken from Tarnopol, 1980, *Jewish Encyclopedia*.

11. Coincidentally, the director Yael Strom revisits the town of Peremyshlyany in his film, *The Last Klezmer: Leopold Koslowski—His Life and Music.*

12. Some details have been taken from the accounts by Seymour Kleinberg.

13. *Tavo* is Hebrew, a masculine form of address (Tec, p. 315).

14. There are various spelling of this camp's name, including Maly Trostenets. It was originally built near Minsk as a concentration camp for Soviet troops captured by the Nazis but later was turned into an extermination camp. The first transport of Jews arrived there in May 1942. Although its primary purpose was the extermination of the substantial Jewish community of Minsk and the surrounding area, many Jews from Germany, Austria, and the present-day Czech Republic were killed there as well.

15. It is now referred to by its Ukranian name, Lviv. It is Lemberg in German and Yiddish, Lvov in Russian, and Lwów in Polish. As noted above, regarding Tarnopol, the names of towns in this region of Ukraine reflect their history of occupation. Prior to 1939, Lvov had a Jewish population of almost 110,000.

16. As of a 2005 estimate, according to a computerized database financed by the United States Holocaust Memorial Museum, there are still about 92,000 Jews in Central Asia. The database can be retrieved from http://resources.ushmm.org/uzbekrefugees. In 1942, approximately 152,000 Jews fled or were deported to Uzbekistan, primarily from Ukraine and Belarus (including areas that were formerly eastern Poland), as well as Bessarabia, the Baltic States, and elsewhere. Also, see the documentary film *Saved by Deportation: An Unknown Odyssey of Polish Jews.*

4

Sh'erit ha-Pletah
The "Surviving Remnant"

> When we left our hiding place one of the first things we did was look in a mirror to see what we looked like. We had not seen ourselves for many months.
>
> —*Betty (Bronka Silvering) Berman*

Today, what remains of the Radegast Station in the Lodz suburb of Marysin is a section of rail upon which an empty cattle car sits, part of a recently constructed Holocaust memorial. In August 1944, Bronka, Lusia, Dorka, and Frania, four girls who had lost their childhoods amidst the harshness, brutality, and deprivation of the ghetto, stood before just such a car, among the deportees who were destined for the camp at Osweicim—we know it by its German name, Auschwitz. On a visit to Poland a few years ago, I stood in the same spot, thinking, "I am standing where they stood. What were they feeling?" Surely confusion, fear, bewilderment. But it was, as a Girls Club survivor told me, "impossible to imagine."

When the girls were forced into the ghetto, they were nine and ten years old; now they were teenagers. "I was about fifteen," Lusia says, "when I left the ghetto." But she quickly corrects herself: "When they took me. They were afraid the Russians were coming so they took us to Auschwitz." The "us" to whom Lusia refers were the remaining members of her immediate family. Of her maternal grandmother's ten children and twenty-five grandchildren,

59

only Lusia, her mother, two of her mother's four sisters (and one of their husbands), and two cousins were still alive.

Earlier that year, in May 1944, the Germans had decided to liquidate the Lodz ghetto, through which, it is estimated, more than 200,000 Jews had passed during its existence. By that summer, most of those who hadn't died of hunger or disease, or who hadn't been killed, had already been deported. The final mass deportations began on June 23 and lasted until mid-July. More than 7,000 were sent to their immediate deaths in Chelmno from the Radegast Station. On August 9, deportations resumed, this time to Auschwitz; the final transport left from Lodz on August 30. As a result, by the end of that month, the entire ghetto was almost emptied of its 72,000 remaining inhabitants (Flaum, 2003, table E).[1]

Camps such as Treblinka, Belzec, and Chelmno were worse than Auschwitz in the sense that they were exclusively extermination camps. Yet Auschwitz, more than any other camp, continues to be the most infamous symbol of the Holocaust. In part this is because, unlike those camps, the physical remains of Auschwitz have been preserved. The Nazis had no time to destroy them; the Russian army was approaching too rapidly for them to hide their heinous crimes against humanity (Bartoszewski, 1991, p. 13). While the despicable practices and conditions of Auschwitz—indeed, in all of the major camps—are now well known and have been described in detail elsewhere, it is important to briefly revisit some of the elements of life there in order to place the women in context: to personalize what, in so much retelling, has almost become an abstraction.[2]

As the world now knows, Auschwitz was actually three camps. Auschwitz I opened in June 1940 and for almost two years was used as a concentration camp for Polish political prisoners, not for Jews. It was conceived as part of the pact between Stalin and Hitler that "contained secret provisions for the mutual extermination of potential Polish opponents of both regimes" (Bartoszewski, 1991, p. 9). With the construction of Auschwitz II–Birkenau, the camp became a death factory. It was in II that the Jews—90 percent of its victims—were killed. The first were women, almost one thousand, brought there from Slovakia in March 1942. It was in II that the majority of Jews went from the cattle cars, which were emptied onto the notorious arrival ramp, directly to the gas chambers; historians generally agree on the rough figure: about 1.5 million.[3] (Auschwitz III, the last to be built, was a slave labor camp.)

The importance of events that occurred "on the ramp" can't be overstated, for it was there that it was determined who would live and who would immediately be put to death. It was also on the ramp that the Nazis "linked the destiny" of women and children:

> On the arrival ramp at Auschwitz the orders were for all children to remain with the women. . . . It is well known that some of the Jews who worked on the arrival ramp walked among the women lining up for the selection and told the young women to "give their children to the grandmother." The workers, who knew that the grandmother—and the children—were already destined for the gas chambers, were trying to save the lives of the young mothers. The new arrivals, however, did not know what was happening—and certainly did not understand the true meaning of the instruction. Naturally most women clung to their children (and many young children to their mothers) and were sent to the gas chambers with them. (Ofer & Weitzman, 1998, pp. 10, 11)

Upon their arrival at the camp, Bronka couldn't understand why her mother was sent in one direction, while she and her aunt were shunted in another; she was in a state of shock and confusion. She soon learned that her mother had been led directly to the gas chambers. "All I could think was, 'how is this happening? Why—how is it possible?'" Bronka concludes, "We were in hell."

In Lodz, as they headed toward the Radegast train station in Marysin, the last deportees from the ghetto thought they were being taken to labor camps in Germany; some even dared to fantasize about a normal train ride to a less brutal place. But once they saw the cattle cars, most realized that they were being transported to one of the camps—and likely to their deaths. They didn't know which camp, but they'd heard the rumors: "We had heard about gas chambers and crematoria before we got to Auschwitz," wrote a survivor of the Lodz ghetto (Feigenbaum, 1999, n.p.). By then, a report prepared by two successful escapees from the camp had been revealed to the disbelieving world; it was complete with details of the organization, apparatus, and methods of mass extermination. Undoubtedly Chaim Rumkowski, the head of the Lodz Judenrat, knew where they were headed as he and his family were deported on the next-to-last transport. About fifteen hundred Jews were left in the ghetto—mostly to work as clean-up crews. Some were chosen by Hans Biebow, the German supervisor of the ghetto, to be sent to work in Germany.

A teenaged survivor of the Lodz deportations described the scene at the railroad station: "The cattle cars that were used were being loaded in exemplary order. Exactly 32 persons were put into each wagon, no matter if anybody's child, father, or mother stayed behind. There was no use begging" (Podolska, 2004a, n.p.).

As we know from thousands of such testimonies, the numbers of people crammed into the cars varied; often people were packed in so tightly it was impossible for them to sit down. It was difficult to breathe, since most cattle cars had only a small window or two. And they had, perhaps, "one bucket, one slop bucket," another teenaged survivor remembered. There was no food, no drink, just "whatever we'd grabbed; we had been saving bread because we were so conditioned that you have to save something for tomorrow" (Ayer, 1999, p. 36). The heat was stifling in the summer; it was freezing cold in winter. Some deportees spent four, five, or even more days in transit: those traveling from Greece, for example, or from the Balkan states. Many perished on the way. Mercifully, the trip from Lodz to Auschwitz was relatively brief.

Lusia won't talk about it: "I was sent to Auschwitz, but I'm not telling you about it," she said. Except for this: "Even when they shaved my head and had me naked, it felt terrible. But it didn't touch my inner being, my inner strength or character." Lusia was referring, of course, to the de-lousing, disinfection routine for those who had survived what has come to be known in Holocaust literature as "the ramp," the first hurdle of the selection process. For teenaged girls of this earlier era, the shame of having to stand naked, mortified, and exposed, alongside strangers, was undoubtedly even more agonizing than it would be today—particularly for the observant, for whom modesty is a fundamental virtue. To make the experience even more humiliating, guards would leer at them and point at them, laughing. "I was consciously detached," Lusia says. "It would consume me if it didn't work."

The girls' sense of disorientation was acute. At first, after the disinfection, with their heads shaven, they weren't able to recognize even their own relatives.[4] Then they were given some ill fitting clothing: one dress to wear at all times—waking and sleeping—and some shoes or clogs. The girls were spared the ordeal of having an identification number tattooed on their arms, the mark of Auschwitz. "I do not have a tattoo," Betty says, "and as far as I know people who arrived in Auschwitz at about the same time I did from Lodz do not have them either." Although they didn't know it at the time, it was be-cause they were going to be sent on.

Conditions varied during the years that the camps at Auschwitz operated, and were different in each part of the camps, but generally several hundred prisoners lived in hastily and poorly constructed brick or wooden barracks. The buildings were not insulated; in fact, if you visit the camp you will see gaps between the boards of the walls so that, in the wintertime, snow blew inside. When it rained, the roofs leaked and dampness permeated the wooden bunk beds, some of which had straw pallets. The barracks swarmed with in-sects, vermin, and rats. There was a constant shortage of water for washing and a lack of sanitary facilities. There was, of course, no privacy. At night, sometimes a bucket served as a latrine. Communal latrines were in separate buildings; they were nothing more than a series of holes in concrete.

The girls were always hungry—an invariable and persistent memory of the camp. Food consisted of watery soup, sometimes with a scrap of meat or vegetables, a few ounces of bread, perhaps a bit of margarine, and tea, or a bitter drink resembling coffee. Already weakened by years of hunger, they were easily susceptible to contagious diseases. The fouling of straw mattresses by prisoners suffering from diarrhea made these difficult living conditions even worse.

As the Russians approached, Auschwitz came to be used more and more as a transfer station to other slave labor or concentration camps farther to the west; for those few, that is, who were not immediately sent to the gas chambers. In a frenzy to kill as many Jews as possible at this late stage of the war, four out of every five arriving Jews went directly to their deaths; the extermination camp was strained beyond capacity. "The gas chambers were operating around the clock, and the crematoria were so overtaxed that bodies were burned in open fields with only body fat fueling the flames" (Auschwitz, n.d., n.p.).[5]

Even for the short time the girls were in Auschwitz, about two or three weeks, everyday life was a struggle to survive. Seven members of Lusia's fam-ily had arrived at Auschwitz. When they were transferred from Auschwitz to a slave labor camp near Hanover, only Lusia, her mother, and her aunt were still alive. Bronka, whose father had died of typhus in the ghetto, lost her mother in Auschwitz. Frania's family had been sent from the ghetto in Pabi-anice to Lodz. By the time the Lodz ghetto was liquidated, most of her family had died or had already been deported; she heard that her father had died in Dachau. The rest, with the exception of a surviving aunt, died in Auschwitz.

"Every day was an unbelievable tragedy," Dorka says. "I went to Auschwitz on August 3, 1944. I got off the train with my parents and sisters—right away they took my mother and little sister. My hair was shaved off the same day." When they were stripped and taken to the showers, her older sister pushed her to the back, hoping she wouldn't be noticed. She was only fourteen; she looked young—small, underdeveloped, no breasts. Dorka's memory is vivid: "I looked at another girl, a sixteen-year-old with huge breasts, envious" because, it was widely believed, survival among teenaged girls was an accident of physiology. Physically immature adolescents, along with children and their mothers, were almost certain not to survive the selections. Lusia believes she wasn't sent off to the gas chambers with her cousins because "I looked a little older," she says. "Because I looked like the right age; the Nazis let me live."

In fact, it is true that many teenagers who "passed as adults" had a greater chance of surviving the first selection. There were also many exceptions, however; many decisions were arbitrary (Dwork, 1991, p. 210). A young child might have been overlooked or might have been allowed to remain with a parent, while a well-developed and healthy-looking teenager might be sent off to the killing machines for reasons that will never be known. Dwork wrote: "Within the construct of the Nazi system of destruction, the role of chance occurrence, of accidental action or timing in the life of each victim cannot be overestimated—both for good and for ill" (1991, p. 260). And not a few healthy-looking women were sent to the gas chambers for reasons that are now well known: they were holding the hand of a child—a child who might not have been theirs or might not even have been a relative. "It was one of the rare historical moments when women and children were consciously and explicitly sentenced to death in at least equal measure with men": women because they had borne the next generation of Jews, young children because they were the next generation (Ringleheim, 1998, p. 340).

In August and September 1944, approximately eighteen thousand inmates were transferred from Auschwitz to other camps. Dorka remained in Auschwitz for only three days before she and her older sister were sent to the Freiberg camp in Bavaria, a sub-camp of the all-but-forgotten Flossenbürg concentration camp (Flossenbürg, n.d., n.p.). Freiberg was organized to provide slave labor for Arado-Flugzeugwerke, the Arado Aircraft Factory, where prisoners were put to work making and assembling airplane wings. Altogether, 248 Polish-Jewish women and girls were sent to work there. The number is known since a record was kept by a camp bureaucrat who noted that the Flossenbürg commandant "assigned prisoner numbers 53,423 through 53,671 to the women" (Flossenbürg, n.d., n.p.). Later, when the camp was closed down, the women were taken to Mauthausen in Austria. Conditions in that camp resulted in the death of 119,000 out of an estimated 199,400 prisoners who were incarcerated there between 1938 and May 1945; one-third were Jews. Remarkably, unaccountably, Dorka and her sister were among the survivors.

Bronka arrived in Auschwitz on August 25, 1944. She made a mental note of the date. Two weeks later, she and her aunt were taken to Stutthoff concentration camp, also in Poland, where they remained for about a month until they were removed once again. This time they were sent to a labor camp near the city of Dresden, which was an industrial center for the German war effort. "Before and during the bombing," Bronka says, "I was working in an IG Farben ammunition factory. The factory was destroyed the night of the bombing." She was referring to the devastating bombing of Dresden, in mid-February 1945, which is still a subject of controversy by historians. It created a firestorm, destroying the historic city center. Afterward, Bronka and her aunt were put to work on the citywide "cleanup detail."

Lusia, her mother, and her aunt were taken from Auschwitz, she says "to a camp near Hanover, in Germany: Hambüren-Waldeslust," a salt mine and slave labor camp. Waldeslust is an area of salt marshes located between Hamburg and Hanover. The camp doesn't seem to have warranted a place in history; perhaps it has been lost in the archives of the war, or was recorded under a different name. It doesn't even appear in any list of the minor camps, but both Lusia and Frania remember it all too well. It was there that they first met, although the women wouldn't say they got to know each other well at that time. "We were there for eight months, but people didn't have time to socialize. We were starving, we had no warm clothes, we were kept like animals," Lusia says. In the bitter cold of the winter of 1944–1945 they carried rocks and bricks, dug trenches, and went down into the mines, 400 meters underground.

Still, their ordeal wasn't over. For their final months of torment, they were taken on a forced two-day march from the labor camp to their next destination: "And then we walked," Lusia says, "they made us walk to Bergen-Belsen. And a lot of people didn't make it because they were starved and they were sick. They fell on the road and they were left there. In Bergen-Belsen hardly anybody made it."

At the same time that Lusia and Frania were force-marched to Bergen-Belsen, thousands of prisoners were being evacuated from other camps. In the closing months of the war, as the Allies advanced into Germany, Bergen-Belsen became a collection camp and was inundated with new prisoners. "In February 1945 there were already some 22,000 prisoners." By April, "with the arrival of prisoners evacuated from the east, there were over 60,000" (Bergen-Belsen, n.p., n.d.). With conditions of such intense overcrowding, with poor sanitary facilities, no running water, lack of food, and inadequate clothing and shelter from the winter's cold, it's not surprising that there were major outbreaks of typhus, typhoid, and tuberculosis. "In the first few months of 1945, tens of thousands of prisoners, perhaps as many as 35,000 people, died" (Bergen-Belsen, n.p., n.d.).

On April 15, 1945, less than one month before the war ended in Europe, Bergen-Belsen became the first camp to be liberated by the British. The British newspapers reported that the liberating army was unprepared for what it found. Some limited descriptions of camps that had been freed by the Soviet Army in Poland had circulated, but the graphic images, impossible to conceive of, had not yet been revealed to an incredulous world. "Inside the camp the horrified soldiers found piles of dead and rotting corpses":[6] ten thousand or perhaps as many as twelve thousand bodies. In addition, there were those near death who were suffering from acute cases of one or more diseases. In a woman's "typhus barracks," only about five hundred had bunks to sleep on; the rest—well more than one thousand women—were lying on the bare floors. In fact, the Germans agreed to surrender to the British because disease was so out of control.

One of the British senior medical officers, Brigadier Llewellyn Glyn-Hughes, made it his first priority to remove the dead bodies from the camp. Mass graves were dug to hold up to five thousand corpses at a time. The SS guards were deliberately made to use their bare hands to bury the prisoners, including those who had died of contagious diseases. About twenty of the eighty guards died later of the diseases.

Lusia, her mother, and her aunt were among the living when the British arrived—barely. "I was just two eyes," Lusia says. She and her mother were suffering from typhus and, in fact, liberation came too late for Lusia's mother: "My mother perished in front of my eyes, four days after liberation," Lusia laments. Lusia also had "a touch of TB," she learned later, but she adds, somewhat wistfully, "Here I am."

Frania, too, was suffering from typhus at liberation. But her cousin, with whom she'd gone through the misery of the war, was more gravely ill. "She survived for only a few weeks; she was too far gone," Frania says. Her cousin, like Lusia's mother, was among the many "living" corpses. More than 10,000, too ill to recover, died after liberation. And, historians say, perhaps a total of 28,000 of the prisoners who were still alive in the camp when it was liberated, died subsequently. Nonetheless, as the BBC news reported, the camp commandant, Josef Kramer, "was described as 'unashamed' of the camp conditions" (On This Day, n.p., n.d.). He was later found guilty of war crimes and, in December 1945, was hanged.

About a week after liberation Lusia and her aunt, and Frania, her aunt, and surviving cousin were among those evacuated from the camp. Prisoners with any hope of surviving were moved to an emergency hospital nearby where British medical students, responding to an appeal from the Ministry of Health, helped to treat the former prisoners. However, since the last of the Germans to leave the camp had cut off its water supply, treatment was made more difficult.

After evacuating Bergen-Belsen, British forces burned down the camp to prevent the spread of typhus, and a displaced persons camp of more than twelve thousand inhabitants was established in German military barracks near the original concentration camp site. This is where Lusia and her aunt were housed: "Frania was there too, but I lost her. I didn't know where she was. We were all very sick, and very skinny, so they took care of us, they provided some food. I remember we used to have packages from England with clothes because we didn't have anything. So I had clothes from England, a dress. And most of us had to wait until we recuperated a little bit because we were not human—we really weren't."

After several months, Lusia and her aunt had recovered sufficiently to leave Germany. Lusia's aunt had always dreamed of going to Palestine, and eventually made her way there. But Lusia did not go with her; she was determined to go to America.

However, there were obstacles. First, it had been arranged by the Red Cross for Lusia to go to Sweden where about six thousand former inmates were taken to convalesce (Weiner, 2010, n.p.). "I was already on the train," Lusia says, "but I got off." Instead, in the newly-established DP camp where she awaited repatriation or emigration, she applied for a special program that had been organized for teens via UNRRA, the United Nations Relief and Rehabilitation Administration, an agency of the newly founded United Nations Organization (UNO), as it was then called.[7]

Frania, who also could have gone to Sweden, chose to remain with her dying cousin. She didn't know what to do; she didn't want to return to Poland and the quota to get into America was fixed, making it a tricky option. There was "a lot of pressure to go to Palestine," Frania said. But she had received word from one of her uncles who had emigrated there before the war. He told her that she would "again be in harm's way." Then Frania's aunt learned that it was "easier to get into America from the American zone." Frania managed to make her way to Eschwege, a former German air force base in the Frankfurt district that had been converted to a DP camp in the American-occupied zone.

Estimates of the number of DPs (as displaced persons came to be labeled) who were wandering across war-torn Europe in 1945 and 1946 vary from eleven to twenty million. Organizations like the Red Cross began publishing lists of known survivors and the known dead. Every day, people pored over the lists with hope and at the same time, with dread, one survivor wrote; it was a "nerve wracking wait for news of our family members" (Salamon, n.d., para. 7). They returned to towns and cities to wait at train stations crowded with people holding up signs or photos, waiting for someone to turn up, or for news.

The majority of refugees, like Frania, were inmates who had been freed from concentration camps by the Allied armies, as well as many who had emerged from their hiding places. But there were many other categories of refugees, including political prisoners, forced or voluntary workers, prisoners of war, even Germans who had been settled in parts of Eastern Europe early in the war. They came from every country that had been invaded or occupied by Germany. Between May and December 1945, more than six million DPs were repatriated. But others, such as Jewish DPs who came to be known as the *Sh'erit ha-Pletah,* the "Surviving Remnant," refused to return to their homelands, fearing what they would find. Many had vivid and painful memories of the residents of their villages and towns, some of whom they had thought were good friends and neighbors, cheering the arrival of the Nazis. Or much worse: memories of their families, or entire villages, being massacred. Others, non-Jews as well as Jews, fearing the Communists only slightly less than they had feared the Nazis, were afraid to return to the Soviet Union or to homelands that had been incorporated into the Soviet Union.

It was initally left to the Allied military authorities to find a solution to their displacement. Later, UNRRA took over administration of the camps. Ultimately, there were hundreds of DP facilities in Germany, Austria, Italy, and other European countries. Many, such as the camp at Bergen-Belsen, were former military barracks. Others had been summer camps for children, or hotels, castles, hospitals, private homes, and even partly destroyed structures.[8]

While there was no comparison with what survivors had endured throughout the war, conditions in the DP camps were harsh, particularly at first. There was rationing, due to a postwar food shortage; health care was minimal, sanitary conditions were usually inadequate, and in some cases curfews were imposed. But immediate basic needs were met; Frania and others who found their way to the camps slowly began their physical recovery from malnutrition and the many other assaults upon their young, vulnerable, and still-developing bodies. Yet both young and older survivors were suffering from psychological problems induced—although the term was not used at the time—by extreme post-traumatic stress. They were often distrustful of authorities and uncooperative—many were children.

There were numerous instances of children who wouldn't extend their hands for food, since guards in the camp had sometimes teased and tortured them by making "sport of throwing crusts and watching them fight for each scrap" (Wyman, 1998, p. 97). There were children who cried inconsolably when they were inoculated; children who fought over food on the table when they entered a dining room. There were children who refused to taste ice cream at a Christmas party. They didn't know what it was since they'd never, in their young lives, seen it before, and they were afraid. There were children who refused to board buses for excursions—they knew that buses took people away, people who never returned.

In the early months, DP camp populations were fluid. Displaced persons, still trying to find out what had happened to their families, hoping against hope that they would find someone alive, moved from camp to camp. But as time went on, DPs began to settle down. Particular groups, usually religious or ethnic, concentrated in certain camps, which took on some aspects of permanent settlements. Camp residents set up churches, synagogues, newspapers, sporting events, schools, and even university campuses.

In the camps, people were eager for love—or simply human contact. Sex with multiple partners was common, and some hasty marriages were arranged when women became pregnant. Most pregnancies, however, were planned, and "DP camps were characterized by a population explosion" (Baumel, 1998, p. 236) as Holocaust survivors married and began to start new families—many "with little soul-searching as a vehicle to combat loneliness and bring children into the world" (Baumel, p. 236). These survivors had an overwhelming need to replace families who had been lost during the war. Also, many young women were anxious about whether they'd be able to become pregnant, since their menstrual periods had been so erratic. Many believed, as mentioned previously, that they'd been drugged and they feared that they had been made permanently infertile. Although the women of the Girls Club were too young to marry while in the DP camps, the same psychological dynamics were still in play later on when many of them did marry.

Many charitable organizations offered assistance to displaced persons, along with a variety of services. It was as a consequence of these services that Betty Berman's aunt was able to find her sister after the war. What none of the agencies could offer, however, were new homes. The problem was with refugee quotas, which were completely inadequate. By the fall of 1946 it was still not clear whether the remaining DPs would ever find homes outside the camps. Almost all of the women in this history spent their immediate postwar years in DP camps. Their ordeal was not yet over.

After having spent two years in the forests with the partisans, Sonia was in an orphanage in Ukraine when the war ended. Somehow her cousin, with whom she'd been in the forest, and her cousin's lover, found her there. Because they were determined to make their way to America, the three of them, along with thousands of others, then followed the Soviet army—from Ukraine, across the breadth of Poland, and into Germany. They stayed in a DP camp in Hamburg for a year until they were able to contact relatives in

America who were willing to sponsor them (Kleinberg, 2002, p. 64). They were finally sponsored by an "American" uncle who had emigrated long before the war—but not, as she confided to her friend Seymour Kleinberg many years later, before Sonia was seduced by her cousin's now-husband. She was fourteen, possibly fifteen at the time.

Basia, who had been in hiding until the Soviet liberation, lived with her older sister in a small town until the war ended. Then they made their way, via a circuitous route—"we walked across a lot of borders," Basia says—to a DP camp on the German-Austrian border, at Bad-Weisental, where they remained for several years.[9] They did not go to America until 1949.

Dorka and her sister, among the survivors when American forces liberated Mauthausen on May 5, 1945, just three days before the end of the war in Europe, ultimately found their way to a DP camp in Germany. But first they returned to Lodz, hoping to find other surviving members of their family.

The logical place for them to begin their inquiries was the apartment building in which they had lived before the war. They were surprised and happy to find that the janitor still lived there. They were stunned when they knocked on the door and the woman, recognizing them, greeted them with utter contempt. "Oh, so you survived?"—Dorka mimics the woman, still offended. "That was what she said to us." Despite her disdain, however, the woman couldn't have given them better news: their brother had been there. He came back to the building periodically, looking for them. "Then we were coming to the building every day," Dorka remembers. And one day they found each other.

Renia, her aunt and uncle—all that remained of her family—returned to Sanok after making their way back from distant Uzbekistan. They found her grandparents' home demolished and no trace of any relatives. Like Renia, many Sanok Jews who crossed into the Soviet zone were sent away to the East. In the summer of 1941, however, Jews who had remained in Sanok, along with others from nearby *shtetls*, were incarcerated in a ghetto—Renia's grandparents, mother, and sister were among them. Those who were able were forced to do hard labor, including work in the stone quarries. But by September 1942, most of the ghetto—close to 10,000 people—had been deported, first to a concentration camp at Zaslaw, and from there to Belzec, the death camp. The Nazis didn't transport the sick or the elderly: they were shot in the nearby forests. In 1943 those who remained in the Sanok ghetto, about 1,500, were also deported to Belzec (Sharbit, 2001, n.p.).[10]

The next stop in Renia's long odyssey was a DP camp in Feldafing, Germany, not far from Munich. It was actually the first DP camp exclusively for Jewish refugees, many of whom were survivors of Dachau. The camp was on the grounds of a former elite school for Hitler Youth which—a small example of justice triumphing—was on property that had been forcibly sold or confiscated by the Nazi authorities, very likely from Jewish owners. As an aftermath of General Eisenhower's visit to the camp in 1945, Feldafing became a model for implementing policy toward Jewish survivors.

Renia lived in a *kinderblock* there, a compound that housed 450 children and adolescents. She says she learned Yiddish and German from a Hungarian friend and was able to go to school again, studying English and Russian. "I was good at languages," Renia says. "I thought I might become a translator."

In 1947, Renia was moved to Prien, to a holding area for children and teens who were waiting for their papers to clear so that they could emigrate to the United States. Sadly, Renia's aunt, having lived through all that the journeys represented—from Poland, to Siberia, to Uzbekistan, back to Poland, to Germany—died in childbirth in Feldafing, leaving her husband with a newborn infant to care for.

Bronka and her aunt were still working amidst the rubble of Dresden in April 1945 when, as the Russians were pressing westward, they were evacuated from the city and forced to join a death march. As they were trudging along an abandoned railroad line they realized there was no way they could survive; there was no food and their only shelter along the way was in deserted railroad cars. People were dropping by the wayside of fatigue, exhaustion, thirst, and hunger. Consequently, they made a brave and fateful decision. Bronka says:

> We did not leave the "march." Rather, we stayed behind, hoping that we'd be taken for dead. There were a number of dead bodies in one of the railroad cars and we each pretended to be one of them.
>
> When we felt safe enough to walk away we decided to look for food and came upon what appeared to be a summer *dacha*. We were quite desperate, with little to lose, so we knocked at the door and a woman answered. She must have looked kind and somewhat trustworthy. We must have looked frightful. But there was no way we could hide who we were. We were dressed in our long coats with a "K" stamped on them. We asked for food and shelter and, miraculously, she offered us both.

She and her family simply saved our lives. . . . it was an act of great courage, for they literally risked their lives to save us.

While in hiding, Bronka and her aunt did not see or speak to anyone. "Food was left for us at the door." It wasn't until the war ended in May that the women learned that they had crossed the border into Czechoslovakia, near Karlsbad, which by then had been liberated by the Russians.

When their benefactors left the summer home, Bronka remembered, they were left behind. "When we left our hiding place one of the first things we did was look in a mirror to see what we looked like. We had not seen ourselves for many months." She was surprised when she saw "a thin girl with curly hair." Surprised not because she was thin but because, Bronka says, "my hair was very straight before it was shaved in Auschwitz."

We know that there were few decisions individuals could make to save themselves during the Holocaust—whether in the ghettos, camps, or elsewhere. They were not in control of their lives; choices, when there were choices to be made, were often between equally negative options. Yet choices were made. While Bronka and her aunt most likely would not have survived without the help of the remarkable family who took her in, it was their decision—their choice to lie among the dead—that enabled them to live.

When Bronka and her aunt finally left their sanctuary, her aunt insisted on searching for her sister. They made contact with other refugees in and near Karlsbad and, with them, made plans to cross the Czech-German border, which would take them from the Russian to the American zone. They "smuggled" their way out of the Russian zone to Fernwald, a DP camp in the suburbs of Munich. Remarkably, with the help of a Jewish agency, they were reunited there with another one of Bronka's aunts. Soon after, Bronka left Fernwald to join a cousin she'd learned was in Zeilsheim, another DP camp. Located twelve miles west of Frankfurt, it consisted of a group of private homes, small two- and three-story townhouses that had been requisitioned to accommodate refugees (Zeilsheim, 2009, para. 1).

In Zeilsheim, like the girls in the other camps, Bronka waited.

NOTES

1. There are numerous websites and other sources that cite details from records that were kept by the Germans on the operations of the ghetto, including deportations.

2. Detailed descriptions of life in the Auschwitz camps are available online at the camp website, or at USHMM.org, among numerous other references.

3. These figures are in Bartoszewski.

4. See Dwork's poignant description (p. 224).

5. By 1944, because such large numbers were being killed, any interruption in the process might have saved thousands of lives. The Allies knew of its existence, and its precise location and purpose—they had aerial reconnaissance photos. They could have bombed the camp or at least the rail lines. To their everlasting shame, however, the Allies refused to intervene.

6. The descriptions that follow were taken from reports in the BBC online archive: On this Day: 1945, British troops liberate Bergen-Belsen.

7. UNRRA was the forerunner of UNICEF and was strongly supported by the then ambassador to the United Nations, Eleanor Roosevelt.

8. See Wyman, from which some of the following is also drawn.

9. The only reference to this camp is on the website www.thirdreichruins.com. It refers to one of Hitler's headquarters that was used as a DP camp in that area.

10. Taken from Sharbit, The Memorial Book of Sanok and Vicinity (Poland). *Sefer Zikaron le-Kehilat Sanok ve-ha-Siviva.* Memorial or *Yizkor* books are unique sources of information on towns whose Jewish populations were destroyed in the Holocaust. Written after World War II by émigrés and Holocaust survivors, *Yizkor* books contain narratives of the history of the towns, details of daily life, religious and political figures and movements, religious and secular education, and gripping stories of the major intellectual and Zionist movements of the twentieth century. The necrologies and lists of residents are of tremendous genealogical value, as often the names of individuals who were taken to extermination camps or shot in the forests are not recorded elsewhere.

5

America

A Home at the Girls Club

In the Girls Club, I was never alone.

—*Renee (Renia Felber) Milchberg*

They waited. In the DP camps, the girls waited for the next chapter in their lives to begin. Ironically, most of them spent their last months—for some of the girls it was years—in Germany, the homeland of their deadly enemies: in the DP camps and port cities of Bremerhaven and Hamburg. In 1949, Basia was the last to leave for America, four years after the war ended. "It was a long time," she says, understating the obvious.

It seemed an eternity. As William Helmreich wrote in *Against All Odds*, his account of survivors' successful adjustment to life in America: "Much has been written about life in the DP camps, the frustration of being in limbo, neither free nor imprisoned. Many had had all they could take of communal living and wanted simply to get on with their lives" (1992, p. 21). Life for many young survivors was so difficult in the DP camps that they remember the postwar years "to be as traumatic as the Holocaust itself, and sometimes more so" (Suedfeld, 2002, p. 5).

In the DP camps the orphaned girls, now teenagers, were still in a state of post-traumatic shock. Their parents and, for most of the girls, their entire immediate and extended families had vanished from the face of the earth: brutally slaughtered, buried in mass graves or incinerated. Few of the girls knew

where. And their childhoods were also gone, also left behind in the ashes of
the conflagration. The "lucky" ones had an aunt, a sister or brother, a cousin,
alongside whom they had survived the ghettos, camps, forced marches, hiding
places, or exile.

Throughout the years of the Holocaust, the girls had had to suppress
their feelings; if they hadn't, they would not have been able to survive. "I was
numb," Lusia told me. Bronka said the same thing. For some time after the
war ended, some continued to suffer from psychological numbness, a kind of
"psychic closing off" (Haas, 1996a, p. 9). Without being able to name their af-
fliction, or perhaps not even realizing it, they were almost certainly depressed,
a condition that was "the most common finding in virtually all clinical studies
of chronically traumatized people" (Herman, 1992, p. 94). In addition, the
girls very likely experienced changes in their cognitive abilities (that is, abilities related to perception, memory, judgment, and reasoning). Certainly their
memories were, at least temporarily, impaired.[1] Some of the women still can't
remember the details of life in those years; they are vague, shadowy images
more than recollections. As Dorothy Rabinowitz noted in 1976, in *New Lives*,
her much-praised study of Holocaust survivors in America: "'I was newborn,'
survivors often said . . . [the phrase] suggested that those who had been left
alive after the holocaust [sic] were not only without a place in the world
and without possessions but also had no past life; the roots and ties of that
life—mothers and fathers, the husbands, wives, children and holdings—had
been erased entirely" (p. 107).

At the end of 1945, opportunities for emigration for the uprooted Jewish
survivors were still very limited. Although their most sought-after destination
was Palestine, still a British protectorate, immigration was restricted. Many
borders in Europe were closed to them as well. And the United States had
strict immigration quotas. The largest survivor organization, *Sh'erit ha-Pletah*
(the Surviving Remnant) did everything it could to push for an expansion of
immigration opportunities, but it had no power, only the force of a moral
imperative; its constituency was homeless and impoverished, unable to make
demands.

While legislation to expedite the admission of Jewish DPs to the United
States was slow in coming, the refugees did have a sympathetic advocate in
President Truman. The president

favored a liberal immigration policy. Faced with congressional inaction, he issued an executive order, the "Truman Directive," on December 22, 1945. The
directive required that existing immigration quotas be designated for displaced
persons. . . . [as a result] about 22,950 DPs, of whom two-thirds were Jewish,
entered the United States between December 22, 1945, and 1947. (United States
Policy, 2009, para. 7)

It wasn't until 1948, after intense lobbying by the American Jewish community, that Congress passed the Displaced Persons Act to admit an additional
400,000 DPs to the United States, about 80,000 of whom were Jews. Although
President Truman protested that the Act was still "flagrantly discriminatory
against Jews" (since entry requirements were biased in favor of agricultural
laborers), it took two more years before the law, which proved to be a turning
point in American immigration policy, was amended. By that time, 1950, most
of the Jewish DPs in Europe had gone to the state of Israel (United States Policy,
2009, para. 8).

When Israel was established in May 1948, as many as 50,000 refugees had
already entered that country—Lusia's and Frania's aunts were among them.
Many, such as Irma's father and uncle, had entered illegally. By 1950, after
opening its doors to all Jewish refugees regardless of age, work ability, health,
and so on, Israel had accepted more than 650,000 refugees.[2] Others had dis-
persed to many nations across the world: to countries in Scandinavia and Latin
America, to Australia and Canada, even to Iraq and French Morocco. By 1952,
137,450 Jewish refugees, including close to 100,000 DPs, had settled in the
United States.[3]

In 1945, at what had become the Bergen-Belsen DP camp, Lusia applied to a
special program that had been organized by the United Nations (UNRRA) for
teenagers who wanted to emigrate to the United States. "I don't understand how
I passed the physical. I guess I had pretty much recovered, but I still had TB,"
Lusia says. "It was a *simen*," she used the Yiddish word for sign, "that I was meant
to come to America." Then, as if to confirm her decision, she had an unexpected
visitor: "One cousin from Warsaw found me after the war. He found me in the
names of people who survived. He knocks on the door and comes in and says,
'I'm your cousin.' He told me that some of my father's family came to America
before the war. He had addresses and one of them was an aunt in Florida."

Of the girls from Poland who would soon come together at the Girls Club, Lusia, not yet seventeen, was the first to arrive: "I came to New York in 1946, August." The ship that brought her, the *Marine Perch*, was a U.S. Navy vessel, one of the many troop ships that were converted to transports for DPs when the war ended; on this particular crossing it carried only children and teenagers.[4] Later, other ships—the *Marine Flasher*, the SS *General Black*—brought the other girls after a week, sometimes two, of travel on the high seas. Sonia and Bronka arrived late in 1946, Dorka in 1947, Renia and Frania in 1948, and Basia, finally, in 1949 after passage of the Displaced Persons Act (Irma had come to America in 1941, shortly before the United States entered the war, on the last of the children's transports). None of the voyages were especially eventful; fortunately, the girls were spared major storms, although some passengers were inevitably seasick.

Food was not particularly memorable aboard ship except for its abundance, the ubiquitous Coca Cola vending machines, and the availability of fruit: often bananas and oranges—very special treats after the deprivations of the war and the DP camps. Some refugees had never seen such fruit before. Tom Lantos, a Hungarian survivor who served in the House of Representatives for almost thirty years (until his death in 2008, the only Holocaust survivor in Congress) recalled his crossing in the documentary film *The Last Days*. Lantos said that when he first saw the fruit in the mess hall he asked, timidly, which one he could have. To his delight a sailor replied: "Man, you eat all the goddamn oranges and all the goddamn bananas you want"—a generous but perilous suggestion. After so many years of near-starvation, many found the availability of so much food difficult to resist, but their digestive systems had not yet adjusted to normal eating.

The ships had libraries, and sometimes the girls saw American films. Mostly they passed the time just chatting, wondering about this strange new land they were going to—what would their new "families" be like, would they be accepted? Some made friends with young men and women they recognized from the camps, or made new friends on the ship—friends, as Frania explained, who would become very important to them: young survivors like themselves, who knew what they'd been through and who could understand their excitement, fear, and anxiety.

Upon arriving in New York, Lusia recalls, "They took all the kids to a special home in the Bronx." The new arrivals were tired, confused, and disoriented, an experience that would prove to be typical, recounted with slight variations by many other refugees. "We were in a strange country," Lusia said. "We didn't know the language, the customs. Everything was unfamiliar." Not knowing the language, however, sometimes turned out to be "less of a problem . . . than becoming familiar with the nuances and unspoken assumptions of the culture" (Suedfeld, 2006, p. 6). Lusia remembers being bewildered when she was served her first American breakfast: "They gave us orange juice. Before the war we had oranges sometimes, special treats. The juice? Never," she says. "And what was corn flakes? I didn't even know how to eat it." Irma tells a similar story: "On the first morning of our arrival all of us were sitting at nicely set tables, trying to figure out what to do with Rice Krispies, until someone came and picked up the pitcher of milk and showed us."

Lusia continues: "Each one of us stayed there," in the shelter, "until we found a place elsewhere." Like other Holocaust survivors, children and teenagers were sent "wherever they had friends or relatives already established in America, or wherever the Jewish social agencies that brought them from Europe . . . found sponsors for them. They were sent all over the country." Many remained in New York City, however: "It was decided that New York would take half of them, a number commensurate with the size of its Jewish population" (Rabinowitz, 1976, p. 105). Many youngsters were excited; it was, after all, an adventure. But they were also wary, fearful, yearning for the familiar—impossible, of course, it was long gone by now. They would be sent to live with strangers, no matter if those strangers were family.

"I had an aunt in Florida, my father's sister, Malka, who I didn't know and she didn't know me," Lusia says, "but she wanted me to come." And so she was sent off to Miami Beach. Regrettably, however, it wasn't long before Lusia was unhappy living with her aunt. And, for various reasons, their first homes in America were difficult for almost all the girls, a situation that was not uncommon. Although social workers who counseled displaced young people grew to respect "the essential wholeness and ability to function of the great majority of those who have migrated to America," they realized that many were unable to adjust to living with their host families (Frankel & Michaels, 1951, p. 321).

Like those destined for the Girls Club, many young survivors felt unwanted, misunderstood, or unfairly treated, even those who were living with the families of a brother, sister, or cousin with whom they had emigrated. One study of survivors found that conflict with relatives "was the most commonly reported problem. It was also a frequent subject of letters to the *Forward* [a Jewish language newspaper] in the *Bintel Brief* [the personal column]. . . . Family problems were often intertwined with cultural clashes and generational differences . . . having family here did not necessarily guarantee that everything would work out" (Haas, 1996, p. 82).

The girls, like most survivors, needed to belong, one of the most elemental psychological human needs.[5] They desperately wanted to fit in with their new families, new culture, and new society. But because their brothers, sisters, or cousins were also newly arrived and trying to establish new lives, the girls felt there wasn't room for them. Others, those who were with "American" families, whether they were relatives or foster families, didn't feel they were in the right place; they felt they simply didn't "fit in." First, they lacked a shared history. The girls were convinced that Americans—no matter how empathetic—who had not experienced the war firsthand were simply not able to understand them. Like so many other young refugees in similar circumstances, the girls had a sense of themselves as different, as "other," a feeling that became more fixed over time. As Yael Danieli, whose career working with survivors spans more than a half century, writes, it was a feeling that intensified their "already profound sense of isolation" (1992, p. 197).

Exacerbating these feelings was the impatience many Americans displayed toward the refugees. They urged them to "let bygones be bygones," to "get on with their lives" (Danieli, 1992, p. 197). Some analysts suggest that Americans wanted the refugees to forget, to move on, so that they themselves could also forget: especially American Jews, whose fortunes during the war were in such stark contrast with those of the survivors. "After liberation . . . survivors were victims of a pervasive societal reaction comprised of obtuseness, indifference, avoidance, repression and denial of their Holocaust experiences. . . . survivors' war accounts were too horrifying for most people to listen to or believe" (Danieli, 1992, p. 197).

Holocaust survivors also suffered from negative stereotypes: they must be cunning—how else could they have survived? Or, conversely, many Americans held a blame-the-victim mind-set—Jews were as sheep to the slaughter, a "pervasively held myth that they had actively or passively participated in their own destiny" (Danieli, 1992, p. 197).[6] Many Americans were unable to grasp the idea that the slightest possibility of outmaneuvering the Nazi machine, given the extremely limited choices available to Jews during the Holocaust, made it remarkable that there was *any* resistance whatsoever. For their part, many survivors held their own counter-stereotypes. They thought of Americans as superficial, lacking depth. Some of the women admit to having felt this way about the American girls they met later on at the Girls Club.

Relatives or foster families were often bewildered; they didn't think they were being unreasonable, particularly if they had the same expectations for their wards as they had for their own children: to share the housework, for example, or to get a job so that they could contribute to the household budget, even if it meant going to night school. It was impossible to know who was actually being exploited. Some scholars claim that over the war years, and later in the DP camps, many young survivors became totally dependent upon being taken care of. Indeed, it seemed normal to many of these displaced young people to accept help "as recipients entitled to be cared for by virtue of their survival and life experiences" (Frankel & Michaels, 1951, p. 324).

As the young refugees began to arrive in the United States in large numbers, scores of Jewish self-help organizations were mobilized for their placement and care. Under the aegis of these organizations, social workers monitored and tried to facilitate their charges' adjustment. They were not willing to risk leaving the newcomers in questionable situations, however, and instead helped them find different homes if the initial placement didn't work out. The girls' social workers, ultimately, arranged for them to live at the Girls Club.

When they arrived at the residence, the girls were still reeling from what has been described as a "triple challenge": their own trauma, the loss of their families, and then displacement and relocation (Greenglass, 2002, p. 1). The ground had just barely stopped shifting under them. They'd gone from the DP camps to living either with relatives or strangers, disappointed to find themselves feeling that they were "in the way," rejected, misunderstood, and feeling disconnected. Unlike adult survivors who "gravitated toward the same communities . . . child survivors were scattered and did not know of each other" (Sternberg & Rosenbloom, 2000, p. 11).

The girls were now part of the *Sh'erit ha-Pletah*, the Surviving Remnant, scattered across the globe. At the Girls Club they realized their good fortune immediately; they had found a home amidst others who were their age and, even more important, who knew the same world they had known as children, knew it as it had been before the Holocaust: girls who had witnessed that world being permanently destroyed but who had survived the slaughter. At the Girls Club, Frania said, she found young women with the same background and interests. She made lifelong friends there.

One by one, during the five-year period from 1946 to 1951, the girls, who were now in their late teens, came to the Girls Club: first Irma, then Dorka, Lusia, Bronka, Sonia, then Frania and Renia, and last of all, Basia.

Irma:

Soon after the *Anschluss*, Irma was sent from her native Austria to safety in a French orphanage, an OSE home. When France was no longer able to offer refuge, Jewish children were evacuated to the United States. Only a few months before America entered the war, in September 1941, Irma arrived in New York on the *Serba Pinto*, "accompanied by American Quakers." She was not quite twelve years old. After a temporary placement at a children's home run by the Jewish Board of Guardians in Pleasantville, New York, she was taken in by a foster family. Although Irma's foster mother was a distant relative, Irma found it very difficult to adjust to living in a family that was not her own: "I had trouble finding my place in it, I was always aware that I was not really a part of it. It was no one's fault. Today we would call it culture shock."

Although Irma had looked forward, once again, to be living "in a real home," she had assumed that her new home—and her new life—would be like the life she knew before the war. She had no other frame of reference since she'd lived only in children's homes since then. When Irma's foster mother brought her to a small apartment house in the East Bronx on that first day—so close to the zoo she could "hear the lions roar," Irma was disappointed and judgmental. She "secretly disapproved of everything about her foster mother," she told me: "The fact that her sons were playing ball out in the street like *gassenjungens*, street urchins to my mind; the fact that she wore lipstick (mothers didn't wear makeup); the fact that the salami was lying next to the butter in the refrigerator, even though I was told that I was going to a religious home."

It was not that Irma was Orthodox, but rather that she felt things were not right: meat and dairy would never have been kept in such close proximity at home. In school she was embarrassed to tell her friends what she'd had for lunch because "in prewar Europe, lunch was a big three-course meal." At her foster mother's she'd have "a lox sandwich and canned peaches with sour cream" not realizing that "probably all the children had eaten that kind of lunch."

Because the apartment was small and the family had two sons, the older boy—although Irma never heard him complain—had to move out of his room to sleep on the living room couch. Irma pleaded with her social worker to be sent back to the children's home in Pleasantville, but was told it was for children who had nowhere else to go.

She now realizes that her foster mother, her "aunt," as Irma referred to her, treated her very fairly:

> She never really scolded me. I always felt, however, that she was holding back, and that made me feel uncomfortable. I felt very guilty and ungrateful about how I felt and secretly kept a list of what I thought I owed her. When it added up to $6,000 I knew I could never repay her, so I gave up that idea.
>
> In recent years, when I began to read accounts by other children formerly in the same circumstances, I began to see that these feelings were quite common.

When she began school in the Bronx, Irma should have been in a higher grade, but was placed in the fourth grade because the teacher spoke a little German. As a result, she never totally caught up with her age-mates. She graduated from high school in 1948, just a few months shy of her nineteenth birthday and finally, Irma says, "I was able to go out on my own." Her social worker, who was affiliated with the Jewish Child Care Association, helped Irma find a placement at the Girls Club. "I remember," she says, "I paid the Girls Club $9.00 per week for room and board, and my part-time job at Gimbels [a department store] covered that."

Dorka:

She lived with her older sister's family when they first came to America but, Dorka says, "I felt like a third wheel." The relationship with her sister turned sour—the sister with whom she had been miraculously reunited in Auschwitz and whom she credited with saving her life there—the sister with whom she survived Mauthausen and with whom she returned to Lodz in search of their brother. Dorka believes that her sister took advantage of her, used her as "a free maid": a story now familiar to the social workers.

Dorka was one of the first of the postwar refugees to move to the Girls Club. In 1942, in the Lodz ghetto, she'd met a girl named Martha. When

Dorka arrived in America, she and Martha were reunited through a mutual friend. "Martha was living at the Girls Club and she said I should move into the Girls Club," Dorka says. "The UJA [the United Jewish Appeal] helped me." Dorka was already living there in 1948 when Lusia, her childhood schoolmate in Lodz, arrived.[7]

Lusia:

Lusia liked living in Miami Beach. "It was so nice there. But I was so miserable because I wanted to go to school. I wasn't even seventeen. My mother drummed into me, 'you have to go to school.' And she, my aunt Malka, only wanted to send me to work in Woolworth, the five and ten cent store." Lusia was terribly frustrated but, at the same time, it was very difficult for her to explain:

> I couldn't speak English, I could hardly speak Jewish [Yiddish]. I don't know how I survived. My grandmother spoke Jewish to me, so I understood everything, but I spoke Polish. I couldn't communicate with my aunt, not much. I couldn't communicate with anybody, really. I only had a cousin who understood what I wanted, to go to school.
>
> And I had social workers taking care of me. I didn't know at the time what a social worker was, but they were wonderful people. They were really there to help us because they knew that we were orphans, we had nobody. So they shipped me back to New York and they placed me in a foster home with a Jewish family in Far Rockaway, in Queens. They're not here anymore.

Lusia had a good relationship with her foster family. They were "good, nice people," she says, although she adds, somewhat cynically, "I think they were in foster care also for the money."

Lusia hadn't had any formal schooling since the fifth grade. She entered high school at seventeen with only the few words of English she'd acquired in Miami Beach—and a dictionary. "I went through all my classes, did my homework, with that dictionary." With the help of a new friend (also named Lusia) and a caring teacher—and by going to summer school and "studying day and night"—Lusia graduated from Far Rockaway High School with an academic diploma after only two years. It was a remarkable achievement. Soon after graduation, Lusia moved to the Girls Club so that she could attend Brooklyn College—too long a commute from Far Rockaway.

Bronka:

Like Lusia, Bronka was seventeen when she arrived in America on a transport from Hamburg; it was December 1946. Bronka's aunt, with whom she had spent the final years of the war and with whom she had been in hiding in Czechoslovakia after they escaped from the death march, had emigrated to Israel. Bronka first went to live with a surviving older cousin and his young family, also refugees. "I had no other family," Bronka says, "no source of income, I didn't know the language. I was totally dependent. And I was still numb." But not totally numb; she was able to feel unwelcome and not an integral part of her cousin's family. And she also felt as if she were an added burden to them since they were immigrants themselves, struggling to find their bearings and make their way. She didn't stay with them for very long. With the help of a social worker who, Bronka says, was "essential in my life," she moved to the Girls Club "sometime in 1947."

Sonia:

Sponsored by their American relatives, Sonia, her cousin, and her cousin's husband, came to America in 1946.[8] Sonia went to live with her father's brother and his wife in Detroit. (Her aunt tried to rename her, but Sonia rejected her American name. Shirley, she believed, didn't suit her personality at all.) From the start, Sonia was very fond of her uncle, who reminded her of her father. But she didn't get along with her aunt, a problem that was exacerbated after her uncle died. Sonia then moved to Brooklyn where she roomed, briefly, with some American cousins, and then moved to the Girls Club for her senior year of high school. Sonia learned about the Girls Club from a social worker, Felicia (Fela) Berland, with whom she developed a close friendship and whose agency was involved in supervising the residency.

Frania:

When she first came to America, Frania lived with the family of a cousin who had come to the United States before the war, "in a big house in Jamaica Estates," a relatively affluent neighborhood in the borough of Queens in New York City. But she was uncomfortable living with them because she was a teenager and they were a young family, with young children. In addition, she says, they were "*shomer shabbos*," that is, strictly observant. Her cousins particularly disapproved of her visiting friends in Manhattan on Saturdays, the Sabbath, because she had to take the subway; riding on the Sabbath is strictly forbidden for orthodox Jews. There was no way her cousins could have understood how important these friends, whom Frania had made in the DP camp at Eschwege, were to her. As Dorothy Rabinowitz wrote:

> The one link with the past was friends they had known in Europe, friends who could remember them as they were. . . . "It gives back a part of you that is lost, that is dead," [a survivor said] and this was a gift without price for some survivors who could never long put from their minds the knowledge that the entire world of their origin, not only their families, had been obliterated. They looked for confirmation of the past in the presence of friends. (1976, p. 107)

But even if Frania's cousins had understood, they would not have been able to accommodate a need that conflicted with their religious obligation. Eventually, her friends helped her find work with an insurance company as a file clerk and later as a bookkeeper. She was able to rent a room from a widow in Williamsburg which, at that time, was still a poor, heavily immigrant neighborhood in Brooklyn. From there, as soon as she was able, Fran (her Americanized name) moved to a large apartment in Manhattan that she shared with other "international roomers," and which they rented from yet "another widow." Her fourth move—"no more widows," she says—was to the Girls Club.

Renia:

Because Renia was quite ill in 1948 when she made the voyage to the United States, her experience was initially different from the other girls. Renia had contracted polio as a child, which left her without the use of an arm. Then she endured the harshness of five years in Siberia and in an orphanage in Uzbekistan. She arrived in the United States with a lesion on one of her lungs, was sent to a hospital in Denver, and was diagnosed with tuberculosis. The diagnosis proved incorrect, but Renia remained at the hospital for about a year, recuperating. From there she was placed for a short time with her maternal uncle, then with a foster family in the Bronx, and finally, after two years of being shunted from place to place, she found a home in the Girls Club. "In the Girls Club, I was never alone," Renia says.

Finally, Basia:

A few years younger than the others, Basia never became part of the clique of Polish girls. By the time she arrived at the Girls Club in 1951, the earlier arrivals were in college or already had jobs. In fact, there were very few European girls at the residence when she arrived and most of the American girls were there as a result of broken homes or abusive families. Basia says, "I strongly empathized with them and felt very sorry for them, but I didn't feel as if we had anything in common." With the exception of Renia, Basia didn't develop close friendships there.

When she first arrived at the Girls Club, Basia hadn't completed high school. She didn't attend Thomas Jefferson in Brooklyn, however. She was already enrolled at Seward Park High School on the lower east side of Manhattan. Basia continued to travel there from Brooklyn because the school offered an English language program for immigrant teens. "I don't know how I did it," she says, "I didn't know any English, I learned by rote." But she graduated and found a job.

Basia spent most of her free time with her brother and her sister's family. "For me, it was mostly a place to come and go," she says. "Still, the Girls Club was a good place, a pleasant place." She was happy to be there.

Irma was the first of the girls to come to the United States, the first to live in the Girls Club, and the one who lived there for the longest time. Not surprisingly, she remembers the residence well and was able to describe it in considerable detail. The following is drawn primarily from her recollections.

The Girls Club, located at 174 Prospect Place, was a large, five-story, gray stone building. Its concrete lower façade was designed to look like large stone blocks. Sets of three large windows on either side of the entry were separated by a large wooden door. Altogether, no fewer than thirty-six windows faced the street.

On the ground floor, the dining room was furnished with a few square tables, each with four chairs. Nearby was a library and two dayrooms where the girls played mah-jongg or cards. One room had a television set, still rare in the late 1940s and early 1950s: "Friday night was TV night." There were also several large common rooms in the residence; special events such as dances—"I owe them my husband," Irma says, "since I met him at one of the dances they frequently held"—birthday parties, even an occasional bridal shower and wedding were held there. Bronka's and Dorka's weddings took place at the Girls Club.

At the bottom of the stairway to the upper floors were handsomely carved and richly grained newel posts. The second floor hallway was wide enough for a large full-length mirror and a bench made of polished dark wood where, Irma says, the girls would "hang around and talk." Nearby was a room where they often gathered to do their homework. The laundry was also on the second floor, next to which was a small room that held an ironing board. Since there was usually more than one girl doing laundry, Irma recalls, "we used to hang out there, too."

The Girls Club had a small staff. Rose Feldman, respectfully referred to as "Mrs. Feldman" by the girls, was the administrator and executive director—and often surrogate parent. Esther Kelner was the efficient house manager, and there were a few part-time workers. Some were women who came in the late afternoons and worked through the evening, keeping track of the girls' comings and goings, signing them in and out. Lucia remembers that "they kept close watch; they were strict. We had curfews on weekdays, eleven o'clock, and on weekends it was between twelve and one."

Volunteers such as Etta Alexander "ran errands" and did odd jobs for the staff. Sylvia Hoffman was the secretary-bookkeeper at the Girls Club from 1945 to 1951.[9] And, in 1949, a social worker, Ruth Schwab, was added to the staff to assist the director as group youth worker. Ruth had spent the previous two years at a children's home in Heidelberg, Germany, working with East European orphans awaiting adoption. But, "I don't think anybody talked about the Holocaust to her," Lucia says, "we hadn't come out of shock yet." Some of the girls think there was a psychologist who came from time to time but who was not a "regular." If there was such a person, he or she did not make a significant impression upon the girls.

Lusia—by now she was called Lucy—had been accepted for matriculation at Brooklyn College, one of the colleges in New York City's university system (no small accomplishment; admission to the tuition-free city colleges was based upon high entrance requirements). Lucy says:

> I had to move from Far Rockaway because of the transportation, so that's when they put me in the Girls Club. There were Jewish girls there who came from all over the United States. They lived in little cities but they wanted to live in a big city, to go to school, or to work and become more sophisticated. Most of them were not orphans, they had families. The American girls came here to advance

their lives and their careers. They couldn't do much in the little cities. And they accepted a few *greener* [greenhorns]. Some of us didn't even pay, it didn't cost us anything. And we had food and a room and they even had cleaning.

Each girl shared a bedroom with two or three others. But the rooms, different shapes and sizes, didn't look institutional. Lucy continues:

For us, the Girls Club was a great luxury; the rooms were always clean, the bedclothes were always clean. When I looked out of my window I saw the Williamsburgh [Savings Bank] clock. Whenever I wanted to know what time it was there was that wonderful clock.

The food was always prepared for us; we never worried where it came from. And everybody was very kind. Mrs. Feldman, when we were sick, she took care of us. It was Utopia.

Irma remembers her first impression of the Girls Club: "I was welcomed in a friendly way, shown around and, since it was dinnertime, I was brought to the dining room. I felt satisfied that I would like it there, and I did." Betty's response to the Girls Club was like Irma's: "At that time I thought my life was tragic. I was looking for somewhere to live, to redesign my life," she says. The Girls Club was perfect. "It was welcoming, attractive. I loved it. I loved sharing a room with the other girls."

In describing their feeling about the Girls Club, the word "wonderful" echoes over and over again. After what the girls had been through, how wonderful, indeed, must it have seemed to them: a truly safe haven. Basia, who like Bronka, also took the American name Betty, remembers "a wonderful place." And Doris (formerly Dorka) says: "Everyone was wonderful." She was delighted by the amenities: a "big piano in the lobby, one of the first TVs, a library, a dining room with two meals every day, and the rooms were cleaned."

Lucy loved that it was a place just for teenagers, "a very interesting place." But, as she and the other girls were to learn, it was much more. The Girls Club was the place where their still-raw emotional wounds would finally begin to heal. As Judith Herman explains, for healing to take place, survivors have to acknowledge the trauma in "a social context that affirms and protects the victim. . . . For the individual victim, this social context is created by relationships with friends, lovers, and family" (1992, p. 9). For the women in this story, none with family to whom they could relate, before boyfriends or lovers entered the picture, the Girls Club provided that essential social context. Yet, at first, "we didn't really have the emotional capital to be generous to each other," Betty (Bronka) says. "There wasn't meanness; we always wanted to be closer. But we were burdened by responsibilities; we had to make a life. It wasn't easy." Developing relationships took time and effort.

It was incredible that, of all the thousands of possible places in the world where they might have been placed by the myriad agencies monitoring the adjustment of young refugees in America, it was at the Girls Club that Lucy was reunited with Doris, her childhood friend and schoolmate. They had not seen each other since 1940, when their families were sent to the Lodz ghetto. And before long, another remarkable coincidence occurred.

A few months after Lucy moved to the Girls Club, a young woman walked into the dining room. Her face was familiar, but Lucy wasn't sure if they had actually met before. Then she realized it was Frania, with whom she had been in the work camp and with whom she had survived the march to Bergen-Belsen. The girls hadn't actually been friends in the camps, Lucy says: "No one even had a chance to talk, to get to know each other." Nevertheless, they shared a powerful bond. Lucy was stunned to see her again: "I didn't know she was alive. How we felt when we met each other again, and we were still breathing! We thought we had no one, nothing. We thought everyone had perished." Frania adds, the memory still vivid: "We thought we saw ghosts."

Frania had already begun night school—first at Jamaica High School and later, when she moved to Manhattan, at Washington Irving High School. Although she didn't receive her diploma, she took and passed the New York State Regents examinations and, like Lucy, was accepted at Brooklyn College. "The girls were studious, intellectual," Frania says. "That's why I went to college, they encouraged me."

Betty (Bronka) hadn't graduated either, although she had gone to Seward Park High School on Manhattan's Lower East Side. (She remembers that she was scolded, inexplicably, for carrying a dictionary.) Although Betty was receiving a small stipend through her social worker's agency, she wanted to support herself. She dropped out of high school and enrolled in a business school instead, later earning a high school equivalency diploma.

The Polish girls formed a close-knit group, with Sonia always seeming to be at the center. Everyone agrees that she was charismatic, a magnet for both girls and boys. Several girls claimed her as their best friend, including Lucy and Irma. Although Irma became friends with Sonia, and with some of the other Polish girls, she thought they tended to be cliquey and a bit snobbish. Lucy admits to this: "In the Girls Club we went into American life. But we had a sense of intellectual superiority over the American girls. We thought Europeans were more serious; American girls were shallow, frivolous. I had American friends, but it was a different level of friendship with the European girls."

Shirley Troutman, one of those American girls, confirms Lucy's recollection: "We never heard any of their stories and what they had been through." (Later, however, as Cynthia Kohut wrote in her poem, "A Meeting with Holocaust Survivors," some girls who were living at the Girls Club in 1952 did share their experiences.)

Regarding the Polish girls, Lucy recalls warmly, "We used to do everything together: go to shows, go to operas, to Lewisohn Stadium. There were always three and four of us, coming and going somewhere." The Girls Club was only a few blocks from many of Brooklyn's major cultural institutions. Eastern Parkway, a grand thoroughfare upon which sat an entrance to the Brooklyn Botanic Garden, the Brooklyn Museum, and the main branch of the Brooklyn Public Library. And it was only a short walk to Prospect Park, one of the great parks of New York City with hundreds of acres of grassland and greenery, forested areas, ponds, a lake, walking trails, and even a zoo. The girls went for long walks in the gardens and park, they often visited the museum, but most important to them was the library, where they studied together. On holidays, "we went to *shul* [synagogue]," Lucy remembers. Mostly the girls talked and talked, although rarely about what they'd been through. "Doris and I spoke some, not much. We knew; that was enough." Then Lucy adds, ruefully, "Not to say that we suffered more than other survivors but we went through most of the hell, the longest of the war, from September 1939 to April 1945."

The girls were, as psychologist Aaron Hass wrote in *The Aftermath*, "filled with questions and confronted with suspended answers." He explained: "Having been forcibly excluded from the human world for a protracted period, survivors felt themselves at a loss when they were readmitted. Previous familiar anchors—relatives, possessions, home, daily routines, social etiquette, community—had been stripped away. And because they were not yet adults when the war commenced, many of life's lessons had not been learned" (Haas, 1996a, p. 100). Girls such as Irma who were in America for a longer time helped the more recent arrivals negotiate the unfamiliar culture. They told each other their problems. They took care of each other when they were ill. They provided each other with the peer-group experiences they had missed in their adolescence. For the time they were together at the Girls Club, they were like family to each other.

The Girls Club was much more important to the girls than any of them realized at the time; it certainly served a significant therapeutic function for most of them. As Herman writes:

> Traumatic events destroy the sustaining bonds between individual and community. Those who have survived learn that their sense of self, of worth, of humanity, depends upon a feeling of connection to others. The solidarity of a group provides the strongest protection against terror and despair, and the strongest antidote to traumatic experience. Trauma isolates; the group re-creates a sense of belonging. Trauma shames and stigmatizes; the group bears witness and affirms. . . . Trauma dehumanizes the victim; the group restores her humanity. (1992, p. 214)

For me, it was a good phase," Lucy says. "Still, we were all alone." The young women—still in their teens—couldn't replace the parents, grandparents, or siblings they had lost. But they did provide each other with much-needed continuity with that lost world. They made it a little less difficult "to reach across the chasm" that separated the past from "an uncertain future" (Kestenberg & Brenner, 1996, p. 144).

At the Girls Club, Lucy says, the young women were able to provide "a transition to American life" for each other, enabling them to face the future.

NOTES

1. See Herman, p. 34.

2. This policy created many problems for the new country. Israel was ill prepared to deal with so many refugees. But for many reasons Israel felt the "right of return law," which admitted any Jew who wanted to live in the country, was necessary. One of the major reasons was that Israel needed a Jewish population to be credible as a new state.

3. United States Policy (para. 9). The last DP camp, a place named Föhrenwald, in Bavaria, didn't close until 1957.

4. Some information can be found online in the U.S. National Archives. However, they report that records of ships used to carry troops to their theaters of operations were destroyed intentionally in 1951: "According to our records, in 1951 the Department of the Army destroyed all passenger lists, manifests, logs of vessels, and troop movement files of United States Army Transports for World War II. Thus there is no longer an official record of who sailed on what ship."

5. A psychological concept that is elegant in its clarity and simplicity, "a hierarchy of needs," was conceived by the humanistic psychologist, Abraham Maslow. He illustrated his idea by means of a diagram in the form of a triangle. The basic needs of food, adequate shelter, and a safe environment form the base of the triangle. After their long years in the war and its aftermath, the girls' basic needs were finally being met. But fulfilling their higher-level psychological needs was more complicated. The second level in Maslow's model, after the basic human survival needs, are the needs for belonging, love, and acceptance. These were the precise issues with which the girls were having such great difficulty.

6. A persistent notion to this day. One student in a Holocaust course which I recently taught told me that she'd heard this idea when she was growing up and believed it was true until she took the course and learned otherwise.

7. The contradictory versions of their first meeting at the Girls Club is discussed in the introductory chapter.

8. From Kleinberg, 2002, p. 65. Many of the following details draw upon his memoir.

9. Coincidentally, Sylvia, now in her eighties, lives in my community of New Paltz, New York. Etta Alexander was identified from a photo by two of the American girls, the sisters Shirley and Audrey Troutman.

AFFIDAVIT IN LIEU OF PASSPORT

REPUBLIC OF FRANCE
DEPARTMENT OF BOUCHES DU RHONE
CITY OF MARSEILLE
CONSULATE OF THE UNITED STATES
OF AMERICA

SS.

Before me, G. McMurtrie Godley   Vice Consul of the United
States of America, in and for the district of Marseille, France, duly commissio-
ned and qualified, personally appeared   Irma STERNER
who, being duly sworn, deposes and says :

That   my   full name is   Irma   STERNER
and resides at Marseille, France

That I   was born on November 7, 1929 at Gmunden, Austria,

That I am ~~is~~ single, ~~married to~~

That I am ~~is~~ the bearer of no valid passport or other document for
travel to the United States because. the French authorities stated that
were unable to provide me with an official travel document
prior to the date on which I must depart for the United Stat
as arranged by the U.S. Committee for Protection of European
Children,
      That this affidavit has been executed to serve in lieu of a passport to
allow   me   to proceed to the United States.

DESCRIPTION :

Height : 5' 1"
Weight : 86 lbs.
Hair :   brown
Eyes :   blue
Marks :   none
Complexion : dark

T. Sterner

Subscribed and sworn to before me this   21st day of August, 1941
1941

Irma's transit paper issued in lieu of a passport. She was eleven years old, August 1941.

Sonia, Irma, Abby, Larry. Jones Beach, 1953.

Lucy and Jonas Pasternak, February 3, 1953.

Lucy, seated far right, and her friends. Seated from left: Hanka, Toby, Renia (Laks), Lucy. Sonia peeking over Hanka's shoulder. Hanka's brother Jack, behind Lucy, and two of his friends. Brooklyn, 1950.

Betty Silvering and Hy Berman's wedding reception at the Girls Club. Girls Club administrator Rose Feldman on Hy's left. Mr. Feldman on Betty's right. March 1950. Etta Alexander, far left. Other guests have not been identified.

Roommates Sonia and Irma in their apartment, September 1954.

Doris (now Wasserman) Izbicka at a friend's wedding at the Girls Club, September 1948.

6

After the Girls Club

Settling In, Settling Down

Sonia left her mark on each of us in a different way.

—*Irma (Stermer) Sangiamo*

Sonia died in 1969; she was thirty-eight years old. Although it was never definitely established, she most likely committed suicide. She died of an overdose of a barbiturate, Nembutal, or an interaction with that and other drugs she was taking. The Hebrew inscription and its translation on her tombstone reads: "How shall we sing the Lord's song in a strange land?"[1]

Because Sonia's Girls Club friends spoke of her with such fervor and love (although I suspected that she had become somewhat mythologized), I realized how important she was to them and decided that, although Sonia couldn't tell it herself, her story belonged in this book. Keeping the wise caution of her husband, Philip Zeigler, in mind, that "everyone you are talking with has their own investment in her, reflecting the role she played—or they would like her to have played—in their lives, and I include myself," I developed a composite portrait from interviews with Philip Zeigler; with many of the women; with Fela Berland, her social worker; and with Larry Ginensky, a boyfriend from Sonia's Girls Club days. In addition, Sonia figures prominently in two memoirs written by her close friend and confidant, Seymour Kleinberg.

Some of Sonia's friends still can't believe she committed suicide. They think her death must have been accidental; at least, they hope so. Three of the men with whom she had significant relationships, however, believe Sonia took her own life: Larry Ginensky, with whom she had a long-term relationship before she married, and which began during Sonia's Girls Club days; Seymour Kleinberg, who wrote extensively about his bond with Sonia in two memoirs; and Sonia's husband, Philip, who says that "it was ambiguous," but adds, he "didn't doubt it." In any case she surely died by her own hand; if not suicide, by an accidental overdose. She is hardly the only Holocaust survivor who came to a point where he or she couldn't overcome his or her grief or depression—two who immediately come to mind are Primo Levi and Bruno Bettleheim.[2]

Sonia's friends agree that she was charismatic: charming, appealing, even alluring. Photos of Sonia show a vivacious young woman with dark hair, sparkling dark eyes and a large, full-lipped mouth, smiling gleefully at the camera. She was very bright, cultured, well-informed, and interesting to be with. She had an infectious energy. She dove into projects—and relationships—with intensity and zeal. And she was well-loved by many: the women who knew her at the Girls Club, as well as others who were associated with her elsewhere. But sadly, as Sonia herself said, "I have everything and more that a human needs to be 'happy' and yet manage to be anxious and upset three-quarters of the time" (Kleinberg, 2002, p. 76).

Those who knew her best talk about Sonia's dark side. She was emotionally unpredictable; she could turn morbid and depressed. She suffered from what we might think of today as stress-induced illnesses—neuralgia, asthma, ulcers—although her stomach problems may actually have been the result of the years during the war when she was foraging for food in the forest. Larry Ginensky says that Sonia told him how "she tried to eat berries, roots, anything that could be digested. One time she saw some wild wheat and chewed on the raw grain."

Some of the women, including Sonia's social worker, Fela, who remained a close friend for many years, describe Sonia as self-centered, even domineering at times. And she was emotionally needy, demanding time and attention. Lucy says Sonia could be manipulative with her friends and lovers: "She used them; she had a talent for getting help, for getting people to do things for her." Yet Lucy understands: "Sonia needed more than some of us did, she needed recognition, so she was very boastful. But still we loved her; she had a green light to boast; there was something magic about her."

Sonia was constantly haunted by the memory of her mother sending her off to the woods when the ghetto was about to be liquidated, telling Sonia, "run, run, don't look back." There are contradictory accounts concerning whether she witnessed their murder, but her mother, younger brother, and infant sister were killed as she was escaping or sometime soon afterward. For a while Sonia dared to hope that her father had survived, since he wasn't at home, but she soon learned that he had not; she was the lone survivor in her immediate family. None doubt that Sonia suffered profoundly from what has become known as survivor guilt, a well-documented phenomenon. Many survivors, not only of the Holocaust but those who are spared during catastrophic events when others perished, may experience survivor guilt.[3]

Yet, painful as Sonia's Holocaust experiences were, objectively, they were not worse than many other survivors suffered and better than some. Betty (Bronka) rejects the idea that survivor guilt alone is sufficient to explain Sonia's despair, or why such a promising life as hers came to such an untimely end. Betty says: "We all have those kinds of memories." Betty's mother was "selected" for the gas chambers at Auschwitz; Betty saw her walk away and vanish, never to be seen again. Lucy's mother died in her arms four days after the liberation of Bergen-Belsen. And so it was for all the women; they all lost their parents in the Holocaust. But, as studies have indicated, an individual's reaction may not be related directly to "the particular circumstance in which the individual was victimized." Rather, the "effects of particular stress . . . will always depend on that person's perception of the stress, as well as on his or her coping skills and defense mechanisms" (Haas, 1996b, p. 17). Lucy intuitively understands that it is the individual's character, intersecting with her Holocaust experiences, that determined her ability to deal with her trauma: "It's more personality than the Holocaust; each one of us had our personality. If they blame the Holocaust for what they are, it's not so. It accentuated the characteristics in their personality." Given a volatile personality such as Sonia's, her experiences in the Holocaust might have pushed her beyond her ability to cope.

"Psychic numbing," a term coined by the influential psychiatrist Robert Jay Lifton when he was working with Hiroshima survivors, is often cited by those who study the emotional aftereffects of traumatic events. It refers to an ability to develop a psychological distance or a feeling of being disconnected from unbearable pain or other intense emotions. Psychic numbing, essentially, is a defense mechanism that blocks out feelings. While the effect may be negative if it is extreme, it may allow time, Lifton says, for healing to occur before survivors "confront . . . what they have experienced and derive a certain amount of insight and even wisdom from it that informs their lives" (Kreisler, 1999, n.p.). In a follow-up study of a group of child survivors forty years after the Holocaust, Israeli researchers found that the defense of psychic numbing helped in functioning and adaptation.[4] Other studies have supported the idea that "distancing ability" is an important personality trait among survivors who have been able to make a "successful adjustment" (Helmreich, 1992, p. 267).[5]

Sonia seemed to have been able to become detached about some events that she experienced in the war. "When she related the stories about the partisan gun battles," Larry Ginensky says, "she told it as if she had witnessed it from a safe distance rather than being in the thick of it, with her life in great danger." Larry, who is semiretired from a career as a clinical psychologist, relates a story that Sonia told him:

> She . . . burst out laughing when she told me how the Jews, the Poles, and the Nazis were shooting at each other in all directions. She said it got so chaotic with everybody shooting at everybody else, that they were even shooting at each other. She related it more like a comedy than a tale [that reflected] the intense hate of a world gone insane.

But Sonia seemed unable to tuck the last image she carried of her mother and younger siblings into a safe repository in her mind. It was a cruel irony, her husband, Philip, says: "This was a woman who had lost everything by surviving and spent her life balanced between the most intense involvement with books and people and the brink of the abyss." She was unable to find the balance she needed between acknowledging her injuries, yet not becoming mired in them and moving on.

Irma, who roomed with Sonia at the Girls Club and shared a series of apartments with her for five years after they left the Girls Club, says that what became more apparent over time was how troubled Sonia was. She saw an analyst regularly during the years that she and Irma roomed together. (It seems Sonia charmed him as well as her friends: "He didn't charge her because he was so interested in her case," Irma says.) And, despite what were apparent psychological stresses and problems, Sonia became a very accomplished young woman who demonstrated great social and intellectual gifts. Irma says: "Sonia had many friends. All the Polish girls in the Girls Club were her friends and after we began to room together, I introduced her to my boyfriend Abby and his friends from Thomas Jefferson and she became part of that group as well." When they were both attending Brooklyn College, Irma continues: "I used to joke that Sonia couldn't go to the library without coming home with a date for that evening. But that wasn't what she would go to the library for; she was a very serious student. Sonia was an English major, very much engaged in her studies. She read a lot and spent a lot of time in literary discussions."

In her determination to complete her education, Sonia was no different from many other child survivors. Of her Girls Club friends, Irma, Lucy, and Fran also attended one or another of the city colleges. The rest studied business, accounting and secretarial studies, or vocations such as hairdressing and cosmetology. Like Irma, many child survivors were placed in "grades below the norm for their age because they spoke little or no English. Yet, most caught up. . . . In fact, despite financial and linguistic hardships, the proportion of child survivors who earned at least one college degree" was actually higher than the general population.[6] The proportion would almost certainly be higher if they were compared with women only, and higher still if they were compared with most American Jewish women of the same generation. This was, after all, the 1950s, a time when women were being told that marriage and child rearing were what they were born to do, meant to do, supposed to do.[7]

In fact, Sonia was well above the norm for women in the 1950s. She earned her undergraduate degree at Brooklyn College, went on to earn a graduate degree at Columbia University, and a Ph.D. at the University of Wisconsin. At Columbia, Sonia studied with an eminent Polish-American sociolinguist, Uriel Weinrich. And while she was a secular rather than an observant Jew, perhaps as a result of Weinrich's influence Sonia became a Yiddishist, an advocate of Yiddish language and culture. Her master's thesis was a comparative analysis of the major Yiddish-American playwright, Abraham Goldfaden, with several European Jacobean dramatists.[8] Philip is certain that Sonia was "devastated" by Weinrich's untimely death from cancer at the age of forty-one—yet "another loss" for her.

While at the Girls Club, most of the young women dated and some began serious relationships; they "kept company," an expression commonly used at the time. But they were timid with boys and shunned sex before marriage. It was a time when girls still feared the ostracism that would inevitably result from getting what was called "a reputation," or much worse, becoming pregnant. Sonia, however, seemed to be sexually liberated, willing to take risks few of the other girls would entertain. Betty (Bronka) says, unjudgmentally, that Sonia "was the only one of us with courage to be sexually active." However, her sexual liberation may have had a disturbing origin; it's possible that she'd been raped during her sojourn in the forest and again in Bremerhaven by her cousin's husband when they were waiting to come to America. Some researchers suggest that survivors who experienced sexual trauma "may experience more extreme psychological disturbance as well" (Haas, 1996b, p. 16).

Sonia's first long-term relationship, which began when she was still living at the Girls Club, was with Larry Ginensky, then a psychology student at City College (and a friend of Irma's boyfriend, Abby). Larry says: "My meeting Sonia came about through one of Abby's discoveries. Abby found a girls' home that was filled with eligible young ladies and was a dating paradise. . . . Sonia was one of the most interesting women I ever dated, and I was attracted to her personality, her intelligence, and her sophistication."

The foursome, Larry, Sonia, Irma, and Abby, became the center of a large group of friends—almost all Polish refugees who had recaptured their appetite for life. Larry was amazed at their energy:

> For people who had suffered such hardships, it was hard to believe they were capable of such jubilance. They were very physical and were always touching and grabbing each other. They gently slapped each other on the shoulder, pulled on one another's hands to bring them somewhere, pushed, shoved, messed each other's hair; all in high spirits and playfulness. They drank straight vodka from a half-filled water glass in one or two gulps and spoke with enthusiasm and deep feelings. Sonia warned me about their unusual ways of greeting, and I learned to accept it; they would hug you or even kiss you on the cheek with every first encounter.

Sonia's relationship with Larry lasted five years. Most of the time, as Larry recalls it, "we laughed together, we played together, we talked into the night about literature, and we walked together." But ultimately they went their separate ways; they had disagreements and arguments that he often thought occurred because Sonia was so opinionated. That aspect of her personality, apparently, didn't change as she got older. Her husband admits that she could speak with such authority, such certainty, that if you disagreed with her, "she always made you feel wrong."

Sonia decided to pursue her Ph.D. and was accepted in the doctoral program at the University of Wisconsin at Madison. That was where she became reacquainted with Philip, whom she'd met previously in New York. "We hit it off instantly," Philip says; "we were intellectual soulmates." Philip was also a doctoral student, studying neuroscience. They married in Wisconsin in 1958, and subsequently left for a two-year stay in Cambridge, England, where Philip did postdoctoral work on a National Institute of Health grant.

At first their lives in England seemed idyllic. Sonia felt very lucky to be with Philip, someone, she confided to her friend Seymour, acknowledging her emotional fragility, "who can gently heal the wounds which are still very, very sore" (Kleinberg, 2002, p. 73). She loved Cambridge, being in the midst of a town that reminded her of Europe before the war—the old buildings, narrow cobbled streets, and the little things such as the string bags she carried to the market.

As Sonia was energized by the intellectual life of the city, people she met there were impressed by her "wit and remarkable breadth of knowledge," Philip recalled. Sonia hadn't completed her Ph.D.; she was still searching for a dissertation topic and, while she wasn't formally enrolled in any of the Cambridge colleges, she received permission to attend lectures and pursued her intense interest in English literature. For a while she was feeling physically well—no insomnia, no stomachaches. But eventually her stormy moods took over, and along with them, various aches and pains returned; she had severe stomach problems—an ulcer, it was decided—and developed "an intrusive facial neuralgia" (Kleinberg, 2002, p. 77). She became constantly ill. It was the Holocaust, she believed, that was the cause of all of her problems. She wrote to Seymour: "I'm going out my mind at the thought of how my whole life has to be ruined because I was once such a long time ago made miserable" (Kleinberg, 2002, p. 78).

Sonia continued to suffer through the remainder of their sojourn until, in 1960, she and Philip returned to the United States, to Madison. By that time

Sonia's medical treatments had brought the neuralgia and the ulcer under control. She was able to sit for her doctoral exams and resume her search for a dissertation topic, which she found in the short fiction of Joseph Conrad. She identified with Conrad. She was drawn to his work, Philip said, "because he was a Pole who had had to make a new life and use a new language." When they returned to New York, she and Philip found a large, six-room apartment near Columbia. Philip had been offered a faculty position at City College, and Sonia was teaching there as well, as an adjunct in the English department.

Philip and Sonia returned to Madison each summer over the next few years. In this way, Philip says, although it was an enormous struggle for her, Sonia eventually completed her dissertation. But just before she earned her degree, she and Philip decided upon another, much greater undertaking: they decided to adopt a baby. Though they'd tried, she hadn't been able to conceive—the irregular periods that she and many other female Holocaust survivors experienced may have added to the difficulty, or may have been the cause. Now that her studies were mostly behind her, with a new therapist, a stable marriage, and financial security, thanks to Philip's growing reputation in neuroscience, Sonia felt ready for motherhood. In 1966, an adoption agency found a baby for them, a four-month-old boy whom they named Judah, after Sonia's father.

In her psychotherapy sessions, Sonia had been told that her basic problem was that, because of her feeling of guilt, she did not allow herself to live a normal life. She confided in Seymour, who was, by then, teaching at the University of Michigan: "His diagnosis was . . . that the more normal things become externally for me, the more I'll be looking for ways of destroying that normality" (Kleinberg, 2002, p. 89). For a while longer, however, what seemed to be a normal life did go on. Sonia had Friday night dinner parties at which she observed some of the rituals of Judaism and her childhood: lighting Sabbath candles, preparing Polish meals. In 1967, Sonia passed her doctoral exams with distinction and earned her degree. She had become a successful "student, teacher, wife, and *balabusta* [Yiddish for accomplished homemaker]." She had many loving friends. But her successes were counteracted at all times by "depression and bodily torments" (Kleinberg, 2002, p. 89).

A few months after the adoption, Sonia and Philip moved to Leonia, New Jersey, a town near the George Washington Bridge, with easy access to Manhattan. They bought a beautiful old house, which Irma remembered visiting. It became Sonia's new passion: "She was very preoccupied with fixing it up. She had learned to sew and showed me the curtains and other household things she had made." She became an extraordinary hostess; the weekly Friday night dinners for friends, which had become a tradition by then, continued in New Jersey and became more elaborate. She was a great cook—something her friend Seymour, who had returned to New York, says is remarkable, "given that she never boiled water before she was thirty" (Kleinberg, 2002, p. 95). Sonia had a wonderful sense of humor and was able to bring together groups of interesting people. And, Irma says, she was a devoted mother to little Judah: "Sonia couldn't stop talking about him." Philip remembers that "Judah was an absolute joy, extremely verbal and the delight of all of Sonia's friends."

As with most things Sonia attempted, she mastered the domestic arts. She had not, however, despite years of psychotherapy, mastered her demons. Despite all her accomplishments, "the darkness became more persistent," Philip says, "and she could be depressed to the point of blackness." Then she would ask him: "What is the point of living?" He was unable to give her the answer she could not find for herself. He finally told her: "You have a loving husband, a beautiful home, an adorable child, all the money you need to travel and enjoy life. If you don't know why you should go on living, no one can tell you."

Nor had Sonia's health improved; if anything, it was even worse. She became painfully thin and tried to disguise it with carefully chosen clothes. Philip says that Sonia "was in pain—physical or mental—much of the time. And the fact that she could be so alive at others is both a paradox and a tribute to her strength." An internist prescribed Nembutal for her painful and atypical facial neuralgia. Other doctors prescribed Nembutal for other ailments; her psychoanalyst prescribed Nembutal, perhaps to help her sleep. She was able to amass a large supply. "At the time," Irma says, "she was in the habit of sending Judah off to preschool, then going to sleep, setting the alarm clock for the time she expected him back, and taking an upper of some kind so she would be wide awake to take care of him." Philip confirms this account, but insists that Sonia was "remarkable with Judah: singing to him, telling stories—then she would collapse again." Her friend Fela, among others, had advised her against adoption; they believed she didn't have the emotional wherewithal to care for a toddler, even one as sweet and docile as Judah was said to be. But Philip disagrees; he thinks "it was only her sense of responsibility to Judah that kept her going through that period."

On a morning in April 1969, Sonia went upstairs to the bedroom; her breakfast was left untouched. She wasn't eating; she was taking too many pills; Philip was angry and worried. By the time he went up to look in on her, it was too late. She was pronounced dead twenty minutes later. There was no autopsy, but it was clearly an overdose or a fatal drug interaction. Whether or not it was deliberate, Sonia's death was certainly caused by an excessive use of drugs. "After all of Sonia's struggles," Lucy says, simply, "she was not able to cope with life."

Her friends grieved over the terrible news, while her death left many questions unanswered. The key question, of course, was whether she had committed suicide; there was no note, no farewell, no way to determine whether she had deliberately caused her own death. Could anyone have helped her, saved her from herself? She once told her friend Seymour, "nobody rescues anybody." Certainly many tried to help; friends and professionals alike. Were all of her problems, which manifested themselves in despair as well as in a variety of stress-related illnesses, caused by what she suffered in the Holocaust? Or by survivor guilt? That she would have been a different person, had it not been for the Holocaust, is unquestionable. But would she have been a contented or satisfied woman? Seymour wrote about Sonia, when he first met her (Kleinberg, 2002, p. 61):

> The war has left her fractured, equilibrium fragile. Her only business is survival; it is full-time work that often leaves her depressed, exhausted, pessimistic: melancholy is her usual mood. It is not entirely clear what she is mourning. Of course she is mourning her parents and brother and sister, but perhaps the grief is even broader. The Polish Ukraine of her childhood, *Yiddishkeit*, all the European past in her bones that make America so foreign, that reminds her daily that this present existence is not what she was born to, that she was meant to be another Sonia.

Those who knew and loved Sonia—there were many—mourned deeply. That she is still a presence in the lives of so many of the women is evinced by the fact that her name, and her memory, were invariably evoked when I spoke with them about the Girls Club. "Sonia left a mark on each of us in a different way," Irma says.

Sonia's painful story is similar to others that used to be cited as the norm for Holocaust survivors, rather than the exception—not the extreme of suicide, but the despondency, the dejection, the depression. "Some survivors . . . were so scarred by the horrors of what they had lived through that they were unable to function normally. While the instances of severe impairment were not the norm, they happened and are part of the story" (Helmreich, 1992, p. 83). Until quite recently, studies of Holocaust survivors underlined their disabilities: The emphasis was on dysfunction, inability to cope with stress. The common wisdom was that survivors were unable to let go of the past. American researchers wrote that survivors were unable to feel they were part of American life; they felt they were outsiders who didn't belong because they were essentially different from Americans.

But most of the earlier research was influenced by the growing interest in research on PTSD and was based upon clinical studies; that is, studies of survivors who were under treatment for psychological problems. Moreover, the studies were of adults, rather than child survivors. As a consequence, "interviews and other anecdotal research" were "susceptible to various biases" (Suedfeld, 2002, p. 2). More recently, researchers such as Kestenberg, Krell, Suedfeld, Helmreich, Hass, and others who have studied child survivors say that the expectation that they "would be predominantly or universally maladjusted" is wrong. Some of the conclusions drawn from the earlier studies may apply to survivors generally, but these researchers claim that many or perhaps most child survivors have overcome the most severe effects of trauma—a conclusion supported by studies from places as widespread as Australia, Israel, and North America. Some survivors do continue to hold onto the past and have never felt anything but "other" in their adopted countries; some of the women expressed these very thoughts. But with the exception of Sonia, the Girls Club women were not psychologically impaired. To the contrary, for most of their adult years they were able to lead essentially normal lives.

This is not to say that recent research, including my own, does not have its own biases and flaws—there is no such thing as perfect objectivity or a perfect sample population. For example, in one of Suedfeld's studies of child survivors, "Life after the Ashes," he acknowledges that his data come "primarily from child survivors whose physical and mental health is sufficiently good that they lived until at least the 1980s" and who were willing to write their stories themselves or be interviewed. He writes: "By definition, we could not collect information from those survivors who were severely or permanently psychologically crippled, nor from those who died earlier, from whatever causes" (2002, p. 21). His conclusions, therefore, have their own limitations. Yet it is fair to say, as Suedfeld and the other researchers cited above have done more recently, that not all survivors suffered permanent damage or disability as a result of post-traumatic shock. Nor do all child survivors exhibit the symptoms of post-traumatic shock—although some continue to show some of the telltale signs, even after sixty years. Yet most, such as those in Suedfeld's sample, and the women who lived at the Girls Club, recovered sufficiently to rebuild good and productive lives.

I once commented to Lucy that I thought it was remarkable that she could have endured what she did and still have a normal life. "Not so normal," she said. "Every morning I had to get up and get dressed and make myself go out to have a coffee." But she did get up and get out, and continues to cope. Lucy's life is not what it might have been had she not been marked by the Holocaust—none of the women's lives are. Yet those girls who became adults at the Girls Club had successful lives by many measures—whether they involved work outside the home or homemaking and parenting.

For the women whose problems were not as implacable as Sonia's, their years at the Girls Club set them on a positive course. They created a social culture in which it was acceptable to let go of the past, to pursue a dream of becoming educated, to follow a career—for a while, at least. Not at the sacrifice of marrying or, even more important, of re-creating a family; those who gave up schooling or careers to start their own families never regretted their decision. On some level, conscious or subconscious, they were aware of "the healing power" that would come "from having created their own families" (Sternberg & Rosenbloom, 2000, p. 12).

Before they married, the women enrolled in the colleges of the City University of New York; most attended Brooklyn College. Judith Goldstein (now Koluszyner) lived at the Girls Club for several years before she returned to Europe to marry a young man who had been her protector during the war. Judith has remained friends with Lucy and Fran despite the fact that she has lived in Paris since the early 1950s.[9] When I visited that city several years ago, Judith invited me into her elegant home near the Trocadero, with its view of the Eiffel Tower just across the Seine. Judith, too, is elegant—stylish and gracious—even in her old age. Photos show her as an exquisite young woman when she lived in the Girls Club, a place she remembers with special warmth. Judith recalled small gestures, such as the kindness of keeping her food warm when she came back from her classes in Manhattan, long after dinner; and making friends with whom she forged lifelong bonds. Although she'd been in hiding during the war, and had not had any schooling during that time, she was placed in the senior class at Samuel J. Tilden High School in Brooklyn. After graduation, and during the time that she lived at the Girls Club, she simultaneously attended and earned degrees from both Brooklyn College and the Jewish Theological Seminary.

But academics was not for all the women. Doris remembers that when she was a child, she used to crawl into bed with her mother. "We were an orthodox family and my mother wore a wig," she says, "but when it was off, I played with her hair. She used to tell me, 'When you grow up, you'll be a beautician.'" And, indeed, while she was living at the Girls Club, rather than completing high school, that's exactly what Doris did.

Renee, who had lost the use of her right arm from a bout with polio as a young girl says, with a bit of well-earned pride: "I was never disabled by it." Renee went to a business school where she learned one-arm typing—by positioning her arm in the center of the keyboard—and eventually earned a diploma in bookkeeping. When she got her first job in the garment district, she was thrilled to get her $35-a-week salary.

Betty (Bronka) dropped out of high school to attend a business school so that she could support herself; she later earned a high school equivalency diploma, and much later still, completed college.

Over the course of the years that the women lived at the Girls Club, some attended classes and some worked; some like Fran, did both. Fran worked as a bookkeeper while she continued her studies at Brooklyn College at night. And, during those years or shortly afterward, many of the women found their lifelong partners. Some of the women married other survivors, some married American men. All married Jewish men, with the exception of Irma. Irma met Abby when he was "living at home in a typical Italian household," to which she was, inevitably, drawn. Abby had a large family;

his mother was an immigrant who had come as a child to the United States from Sicily. His father, the youngest of ten children, was born in America, but the rest of his family had emigrated from southern Italy. Irma knows she was very lucky that the family welcomed her wholeheartedly into the fold despite the fact that she was a Jew. Intermarriage was not yet commonplace in the 1950s among either Jewish or Italian families, who often had either anti-Gentile or anti-Semitic biases.

Generally, women such as Irma, Betty (Bronka), and Fran, all of whom married American men, had the immediate satisfaction of becoming part of an established family, with all the benefits that bestows upon a young couple, especially when they begin having their own children. These women had supportive networks during their early married lives that were particularly important to them when their children were young. There were grandparents to transmit the family lore and to love the children in the special way grandparents do. There were family gatherings with aunts, uncles, and cousins for the children to look back upon when they were older—all the normal things, and undoubtedly some of the not-so-normal things, that extended families offer.

Although the Girls Club gave them the opportunity to meet American men, Lucy, Doris, Renee, and Betty (Basia) married survivors. In fact, most Holocaust survivors (about 80 percent) married other survivors. For some, it was the language barrier that made them uncomfortable with Americans but, much more important, "survivors were often, because of shared wartime experiences and a common cultural background, simply more comfortable with each other" (Haas, 1996a, p. 120). Lucy says that she could "never have married someone who was not a survivor."

Such a choice had a number of consequences. First, survivor-to-survivor marriages meant that the women were deprived of the extended families they might have become part of had they married American men. Also, survivor couples tended to settle in communities where there were relatively large numbers of other survivors. However well-intentioned they might have been, neighbors who themselves had no older family role models became inadequate surrogate families for each other. Consequently, "as a group" they did not readily "assimilate into mainstream American society," which, in turn, "enhanced their sense of uniqueness and the belief that only other survivors could really understand what they had been through" (Helmreich,

1992, p. 73). Finally, "partners in such marriages often reinforced feelings of persecution and victimization in each other, and an unusual quality of mutual dependence or protectiveness frequently ensued" (Haas, 1996b, p. 10). What they did have was important to them: the consolation of a mutual understanding of the Holocaust, which they couldn't have had with Americans. The women's dreams of reconstructing a complete family of their own were ultimately realized in their grandchildren and by now, for some, great-grandchildren.

Most of the women remained in the New York area during the early years of their marriages and kept in touch with the friends they had made at the Girls Club. Irma was an exception. After she earned her undergraduate degree in 1952, she applied for a job as a German translator. Even before she had an interview she was asked if she could type: "Who's gonna hire you as a translator, and then get someone to type your stuff at twice the cost?" Since, as it happened, Irma couldn't type, she enrolled in a secretarial course and began working for a wine import firm: "Monsieur Henri Wines" she says, "Monsieur Henri, alias Henry Feinman." She and Abby were engaged by this time and she was teased by friends, not too subtly, about the forthcoming intermarriage: "'He's gonna have you slaving over a hot stove cooking spaghetti all day,' they said. And some people told me I would regret it. 'The first little fight you have, he's gonna call you a dirty Jew.'" None of those predictions came to pass.

After a while, when Irma realized that neither her newly acquired secretarial skills nor her liberal arts degree was going to help her land a professional job, she applied to the master's degree program at Columbia University's School of Library Service. Meanwhile, Abby had been accepted into the Yale University School of Art, and the couple moved to New Haven. Irma says: "We got married in August 1954, in the afternoon, right after my final exams." She continued to work on her library degree by commuting to Columbia one night a week and finished her last course the following summer. During that time she found work as a preprofessional in the Yale Library cataloguing department while Abby attended classes.

In September 1956, they moved to Baltimore, where Abby had obtained a teaching position at Morgan University. In 1960 he joined the faculty of the Maryland Institute College of Art, and Irma got a job as a reference librarian at the Central Branch of the Enoch Pratt Free Library. Once they paid off their school debts, "tiny by today's standards," Irma says, they took a five-month vacation in Europe, visiting places in Italy and Austria where their families had lived. In between pregnancies, and while her two children were growing up, Irma was "preoccupied with their activities, did a lot of chauffeuring them around . . . took camping trips in the summers." But she did work part time, and "on and off," at the library of the Maryland Institute School of Art. Irma didn't return to full-time work until 1988, when she became head research librarian at the Institute, a position she held until her retirement in 2004. Abby still teaches at the Institute. His most recent five-year contract will allow him to retire at age eighty-two. Irma and Abby have two sons; one is an attorney and the other a paralegal—and they have five grandsons.

Renee moved away from New York when she married Irving Milchberg. During the war Irving was known as "Bull," the leader of a gang of Jewish youth. They sold cigarettes in one of the central areas of Warsaw, the Three Crosses Square, right under the noses of, and to, their Nazi occupiers (Ziemian, 1977). At first, Irving boldly walked out of the ghetto in the mornings with other day workers and returned with them at night. But after the ghetto was destroyed, Irving lived on the streets, in attics, surviving under the protection of courageous Poles and Jews. When the war ended, Irving made his way to Canada, first living in Nova Scotia—"the Canadians were trying to spread the Jews out throughout Canada," Irving told Renee—and finally settling in Niagara Falls.

Renee and Irving met during a vacation trip she took to Montreal and were married soon afterward, in 1955. Renee has lived a productive life. Irving ran a successful souvenir shop until his recent retirement. Renee, with her secretarial and bookkeeping skills, managed the office. When the care of her young children allowed, she was involved in volunteer work with Hadassah, and was the president of the Sisterhood at their *shul*. Renee never lost her faith; she kept a kosher home and observed Jewish traditions. "God had nothing to do with the Holocaust," she told me.

Renee and Irving have two children and three grandchildren. Their son is a physicist, their daughter an architect. In their retirement, they live comfortably in Thornhill, a Toronto suburb, during most of the year, and in Florida during the winter.

Lucy, Fran, Doris, and Betty (Basia) remained in the New York area throughout their adult years—in Brooklyn, Long Island, or nearby New Jersey. They enjoyed relatively middle-class lives; they were stay-at-home moms when their children were in school, and then saw them off to college and to semiprofessional or professional careers. Sometimes Fran worked in the office of her husband's successful printing business. Some did volunteer work, often connected with their synagogue or Jewish-related causes such as support of Israel. Because the Holocaust gave a final impetus to the establishment of a Jewish homeland, Israel's existence has a special meaning for the women—for survivors in general.

When their families were young, some of the women spent summers together at Catskills resorts. They also traveled; a few visited Poland, so changed from the days of their youth. Some went back to the camps where they had seen their parents and relatives for the last time, now museums or memorials. Revisiting the camps was as close to the Jewish rituals of grieving, as close to closure, as they could come. They also visited Israel, to which some of the women's families had emigrated before or just after the war.

The lives of these women of the Girls Club, so similar to many Jewish-American middle-class women of their generation, were unremarkable in many respects. But they were quite remarkable given what the women had endured: "They challenged the stereotype" (Suedfeld, 2002, p. 11). The women have some "vulnerabilities" that are a "direct legacy of the Holocaust trauma." But, like other child survivors, they were "determined to build a future for themselves and their families" (Sternberg & Rosenbloom, 2000, pp. 12–13). And they did.

The women whose stories are told here have many similarities. With the exception of Irma, all were from Poland and—remembering that Jewish society in prewar Poland was quite diverse—shared the broad aspects of a common culture. They suffered unimaginable hardship, deprivation, and massive losses during the Holocaust. They made their way through war-torn Europe, most stopping at DP camps, before they were able to come to America. They had unhappy, or at least unsatisfactory, experiences in the homes of their "American" relatives before they found succor at the Girls Club. Almost all of the women finished high school, despite many lost years of schooling, and some pursued further studies. Compared with their contemporaries in North America (that is, in the United States and Canada), a disproportionate number went on to college to complete undergraduate and graduate degrees (Suedfeld, 2002, p. 12). During their adult years they married, achieved middle-class status, and raised children who now have careers or professions and families of their own. For women of their generation, even without taking their experiences in the Holocaust into account, using culturally and historically appropriate criteria, the women led successful lives. Now in their late seventies and early eighties, the women are drawing upon all their resources in coping with the challenges of old age.

As researchers of human behavior know, generalizations can prompt "a selective blindness to individual differences, a leveling to a common denominator, oversimplification" (Haas, 1996b, p. 20). As a result, in this particular history, it is possible to lose sight of the fact that each woman has her own, distinct personality—and her own separate, personal history. Although all the women in this study have many things in common, their lives in many other respects have had very different trajectories—none more so than Betty's (Bronka) and Lucy's. The following chapter, a closer look into the life histories of these two women, illustrates how similar they are, and also how unique.

NOTES

1. The question was asked by an exile from Jerusalem who had suffered many years in Babylonian captivity and was followed with: "By the rivers of Babylon, there we sat down, yea, we wept, when we remembered Zion."

2. Although elderly Holocaust survivors are thought to be in a high-risk category for suicide, there has been no systematic assessment of suicide rates in survivors overall (Barak). Some sources claim that the rate is surprisingly low (Rosenbaum).

3. See Hass (1996b, p. 10) for a brief but quite comprehensive explanation of the phenomenon.

4. Reference is to the study by Mazor et al. in Sternberg & Rosenbloom.

5. A longitudinal study conducted by Kestenberg & Brenner (1996) established that many child survivors showed amazing strength and resilience. Among them are successful scientists, artists, professionals, and business people. Several of the interviewees were chronically depressed—a sign of incomplete mourning and

unacknowledged anger, not a manifestation of clinical depression. Also, Helmreich lists personality traits, at least some of which were present in those in his study who made a successful adjustment. In addition to "distancing ability," he includes "flexibility, assertiveness, tenacity, optimism, intelligence, group consciousness, assimilating the knowledge that they survived, finding meaning in one's life, courage" (p. 267).

6. Research cited by Suedfeld (2002, p. 13).

7. This issue will be discussed further in the following chapter.

8. Goldfaden (1840–1908), born in Russia, was a prolific Hebrew and Yiddish playwright, the author of four hundred plays. When Russian authorities banned Yiddish theater in 1883, Goldfaden left his homeland to found Yiddish troupes in Paris, London, and New York City. He settled in New York in 1903 and opened a drama school.

9. I didn't include Judith in this study, although she was part of the group of Polish girls when she lived at the Girls Club, because she moved back to Europe in the early 1950s, and I had the opportunity for one only brief interview when I happened to be in Paris a few years ago.

7

Betty and Lucy

Different Forks in the Road

I told myself, everything bad that could have happened to me, did. But I'm strong, and can make a good life for myself.

—*Betty (Bronka Silvering) Berman*

Betty (Bronka) and Lucy were born, just months apart, in 1929. They were children, not quite ten years old when the Germans invaded Lodz. By the time they met at the Girls Club they had already lived curiously parallel lives. Although Betty describes her family as much poorer than Lucy's, their fathers were both shopkeepers. Their mothers worked outside the home: Betty's mother worked part-time in her husband's grocery store; Lucy's mother was a teacher. The girls and their families were removed from their homes in 1941 and remained in the ghetto until August 1944. When the ghetto was liquidated, the girls and their surviving relatives—by then both Lucy's and Betty's fathers were dead—were deported to Auschwitz, and from there they were sent to Germany as slave laborers. By the time the war ended they had lost their mothers as well and almost all of their extended families.

After liberation in May 1945, each girl clung to the maternal aunt with whom she'd survived the terror of the war and the Holocaust. Lucy was devastated that her mother, having survived through the liberation of Bergen-Belsen, died shortly afterward. Mercifully, her mother's youngest sister, Zosia, was still alive. Around the same time, Betty and her Aunt Genia, the youngest of her mother's four sisters, came out of hiding in Czechoslovakia. When Zosia and Genia emigrated to Israel, Lucy and Betty decided to part from their aunts and go to America—yet another coincidence.

Betty went to New York City with a cousin with whom she'd been reunited in Zeilsheim, a DP camp near Frankfurt. He was older, married, and had been living in the Zelsheim camp with even more-distant cousins, who took Betty in as well. In December 1946, not long after Betty arrived in the camp, her cousin learned that he and his family would be able to emigrate to America. He urged Betty to come with him and his family. She was easily convinced, she thinks, for several reasons.

In Zeilsheim, Betty had taken a job at an UNRRA office and met a number of other young people there. They became protective of her, as the youngest of the group. Some with whom she developed close relationships and who would become lifelong friends had decided to emigrate to America. Others were going to Israel, but "I was always pragmatic," Betty says. "I believed I would have an easier life in America." She had already suffered so much hardship and disruption, loss, and grief in her young life: "I had enough to cope with." Added to this was the adolescent bravado of a sixteen-year-old wanting to assert her independence. Betty decided, consequently, that it was time to make a break from her aunt.

Soon after they arrived in America, Betty's cousin found an apartment in Brooklyn, near Prospect Park. But it was a crowded household of several adults—her cousin's wife had two surviving sisters who also lived with them—and an infant. "I felt as if I was in everybody's way," Betty says.

In 1947, several months after Betty had arrived in Brooklyn, a social worker from the relief and resettlement agency HIAS arranged for her to live at the Girls Club. Betty moved in and dropped out of Seward Park High School, where she'd been enrolled in a special program for immigrant youth. She wanted to complete high school and go on to college, but she was determined to support herself. To supplement the small allowance she was given by the agency, she took a job in the garment industry as a sewing machine operator, and then enrolled in secretarial school. When she got her first secretarial job, her employer proved to be kind and patient, and she gave it her best effort. However, there was a problem: the English language. Betty could read and write, she says, "but my English was too limited for secretarial work." Over time, she acquired the necessary fluency.

Betty had made many friends among the American residents at the Girls Club and was living happily there by the time the other European girls began to arrive. Betty remembers: "How fantastic it was that we spoke Polish to each other! And we'd had common experiences." Betty was drawn to Sonia, as so many were, but they never became close: "She was aloof, difficult to get to know." She did become friends with Fran; they still keep in touch with each other. And she and Lucy became good friends as well. Lucy remembers her early impression of Betty: "Very intellectual; she played the piano and she read *The New York Times*." (Recently, Lucy was amused to hear that Betty, who lives in Minneapolis, is still an avid *Times* reader.)

Everyone at the Girls Club "was very busy," Betty says. Some, like Betty, had jobs and commuted to work in "the city" (as Manhattan is known to those in the outer boroughs). Others were occupied with their schoolwork. But "we lived together, we saw each other every day at meals." And Betty loved spending time with the European clique. "We walked in the park; sometimes we went rowing." Yet, she says, "truthfully, I was envious because I wanted so much to go to school."

Neither Betty nor Lucy were happy in their first homes in America. Betty felt she was "in the way." Lucy, who had been sent to Florida, had a major conflict with her aunt over resuming her education. Ultimately, Lucy's social worker arranged for her to be taken into foster care in New York. In 1949, when she graduated from Far Rockaway High School, Lucy moved to the Girls Club so that she would be closer to Brooklyn College.

As discussed earlier, neither Betty nor Lucy's problem was unusual. What was unusual, however, was that they found such an exceptional alternative. Betty, who is not given to hyperbole, says: "It is impossible to overestimate how important the girls were to me. It was like life and death." Lucy's description is different, but she agrees: "The European girls had a feeling of connection. Yes, absolutely, that was number one. Even if we were not aware of it at the time, that's what it really was. We were connected."

Their connection at the Girls Club, the sense of security that came from belonging to what Lucy called their "substitute family," made it possible for the girls to bring closure to an interrupted adolescence: to establish their identities; to explore and test out their values; to make new attachments; to become more self-assured; to prepare themselves for intimacy. Essentially it enabled them to take the time they needed to learn who they had become, to get to know themselves, to think about how they wanted to live their lives—and, above all, to move on to the next phase of their lives as young adults. Lucy sums it up: "For me it was a wonderful transition into my next step in life, which was marriage; it was really good."

It was during these important late-teenage years at the Girls Club that Betty and Lucy's lives finally intersected and they became friends. But it was also during their Girls Club years that they began to take very different paths. Although both Betty and Lucy have lived satisfying, full lives, the stories of no two women in this study provide a sharper contrast than theirs. Lucy committed herself to building and raising a large, devoutly Orthodox family. Betty, a cultural-secular Jew, lived the life of a faculty wife while pursuing many interests of her own and, albeit belatedly, enjoying a successful career. Highlighting the contrast is important. Betty and Lucy's life stories are a reminder that, while generalizations may be necessary for a variety of reasons—for example, they enable us to understand concepts that apply to most, if not to all, individuals—survivors are no more alike than members of any other large group of people. Yet, obvious as this may be, identifying someone as a Holocaust survivor continues to evoke certain stereotypical images.

Like all survivors, Betty and Lucy were each affected differently by their Holocaust experiences because of many issues.[1] Individual personality is the most obvious distinguishing characteristic among survivors. But also of great significance is the fact that survivors experienced the Holocaust in vastly differing contexts: in the camps, in slave-labor programs, in the ghettos; hidden, passing as Aryans, protected by non-Jews. In addition, survivors were affected differently due to age, gender, educational level, marital status, and economic and social status—all the things that make us different from each other. Still, the designation "Holocaust survivor" prompts assumptions that became fixed in large part as a result of early clinical studies: studies (as discussed in the previous chapter) that predicted that survivors—in general and certainly child survivors—were expected to be troubled and unable to cope with life.

Child survivors were supposed to have been psychologically damaged beyond recovery by circumstances they could neither understand nor control. However, as a child survivor in Peter Suedfeld's study, "Life after the Ashes," insisted: "We are not the psychologically and socially crippled group that some people, including many mental health professionals, expected us to be" (2002, p. 15). Suedfeld, who is also a child survivor and was hidden in a convent during the war, agrees. His research, and other recent scholarship, supports his claim: "The expectation that child survivors would be predominantly or universally maladjusted is simply wrong . . . many, perhaps most, have overcome the most severe effects of trauma and have been leading essentially normal lives" (2002, p. 22). Suedfeld quotes colleagues who studied child survivors of Buchenwald; he believes their comment applies equally to the entire cohort: "Who could have thought so many would succeed against such overwhelming odds?" (2002, p. 22).

It is undeniable that all of the women whose histories are told here *have* succeeded against overwhelming odds. But "success"—if not exclusively, than primarily—assumes academic achievement or accomplishments in business or in other professions. As the concept of career is commonly understood, homemaking, which includes parenting, is not included.[2] When we evaluate "success" for most women of the Girls Club generation, we have to remind ourselves to think in terms of a broader definition. Homemaking was the career that women chose—given the limited choices available to women in the 1950s—if they could afford not to find paid work. It was also the career that was chosen by most young women who survived the Holocaust, at least in the early years of their marriages.

It is well-documented that "the urge to marry and raise a family as fast as possible was a paramount desire among both male and female Holocaust survivors, many of whose entire families had perished during the war" (Baumel, 1998, p. 236). Men no less than women wanted and needed the singular feelings of connection and belonging, the intimacy that only family can offer. But while the men saw to providing for the family's material needs, the women were expected to commit themselves to building and nurturing their new families. It was a task they took on willingly, but it unavoidably limited the women's ability to also pursue careers outside the home.

Jewish cultural values also pushed young female Holocaust survivors toward homemaking and away from the notion of having careers outside the home, intensifying their drive to settle down and replace their lost families. In traditional Jewish culture, separation of the sexes into different realms— public and domestic—is manifest in both concept and practice. Even in the United States, with the growing secularization of American Jews throughout the twentieth century, the expectation that women's work was within the home has been tenacious. The image of the ideal homemaker, the *baleboste*,

which was brought to America by Eastern European immigrants, still dominated Jewish-American culture in the years after the war. And while few of
the women at the Girls Club espoused traditional attitudes—several had been
raised in secular or progressive homes—social pressure is difficult to resist.

What's more, traditional Jewish cultural values were reinforced by the
American culture of the late 1940s and 1950s. As we know, in order to replace
the men who had gone into military service during the war years, the worlds
of many women had expanded to include life and work outside the home—
not just in offices but also in factories. Now that the men had returned, Rosie
the Riveter was expected to devote herself, once again, to being a competent
homemaker and helpmate to her husband—not competing with him in the
workforce. And, adding a political dimension to the personal in the cold war
climate of the post–World War II years, American society was said to depend
upon the bedrock of the "normal" American family.[3]

It was against this social-historical and psychological background that both
Lucy and Betty made critical life choices.

Lucy is very bright. Despite having missed so many years of formal education, despite difficulty with a totally new and unfamiliar language, she completed high school in two years. Her excellent grades and academic diploma
entitled her to apply to the colleges in the City University system. When she
was accepted at Brooklyn College, she moved to the Girls Club so that she
would be within reasonable commuting distance of the school. She and the
other "college girls" at the Girls Club were serious and committed students.
Lucy attended Brooklyn College for three years; she studied psychology,
thinking she'd pursue a career in social work. Then, abruptly, she dropped
out.

It was 1952; Lucy had been living at the Girls Club for three years. All the
girls were happy there, but "we were still all alone," she says. For Lucy, as for
other survivors, nothing "could substitute for the warmth and genuine acceptance that [they] so desperately wanted and sought" and which, they believed,
could only be provided by a family of their own (Helmreich, 1992, p. 261).
Lucy expresses it in this way: "I made a conscious choice. I didn't finish [col-
lege] because I had no home, and I had nobody, and I thought it's important
for me to have somebody. When I met my husband, I wanted a family, to have
a home already. It was time. I needed to have a home."

At the Girls Club, Lucy was introduced to Jonas Pasternak by his younger sister, Betty (Basia). Although Lucy had dated other young men, and some had been interested in pursuing a serious relationship, it wasn't until she met Jonas that she believed she'd met the man who was right for her. In addition to the personal attraction, Jonas had two things in his favor that her other suitors couldn't rival; he was Polish and he was a survivor. He'd experienced the destruction of Jewish life in Tarnopol; his own parents were among the Jews who'd perished there. Yet he was able to save both Basia, his junior by almost ten years, and his older sister. When the ghetto was liquidated, it was Jonas who arranged for them to remain in hiding, in a variety of rooms concealed behind false, hastily-constructed walls. And when their final hiding place was exposed, it was he who arranged for refuge in the cellar of a Polish woman who had been known to his parents (Pasternak, n.d., n.p.). It was not until 1949, after almost four years of wandering around Europe, then settling in a DP camp on the Austrian-German border, that Jonas and his two sisters were able to emigrate to America.

Betty adored her brother and, appropriately, gave Jonas full credit for having saved her life. Lucy says, "Basia, I mean Betty, came into the Girls Club one day and she never stopped talking about him. When he came once to pick her up, she introduced us. And then I married him."

It would have been impossible for Lucy to marry an American. "I couldn't have married a non-survivor," Lucy says. "There is a song with a lyric, 'we think the same thoughts.' If I were to do it over, I would marry a survivor." Although she could rarely bring herself to talk about her experiences, Lucy had to have a partner who could identify with them—experiences, she believed, that someone who hadn't been through them could never fully comprehend, no matter how much empathy they might have. Lucy believes: "We are all different people, Holocaust survivors, but we know what we are. I recognize them on the street. We're so attached, like brothers and sisters. And we always feel different from others."

Lucy didn't understand survivors who wanted to marry Americans. She thought it was so that "they could become American themselves—leave the other half behind." She thought they were "in denial." If someone "has a number on her arm from Auschwitz," she asks, "how can she be an American? I could never understand." Not that Lucy was antagonistic to Americans. Not at all. Lucy admired them for having more "freedom in thinking" and expressing their ideas. For being "more liberal, accepting of new things." But she was more comfortable with Europeans. We had a "different mentality," she says. Like Lucy, most survivors (83 percent) married other survivors (Helmreich, 1992, p. 121).

In many respects, Lucy's early married life was not very different from that of other young, married, Jewish-American women of the 1950s. And it was certainly typical of survivors of her age and generation: "For the period stretching from the late 1940s through the 1970s survivors were busy. They raised their children, worked diligently" (Haasa, 1996, p. 102). During those years, Lucy says: "We lost so much, we thought we had to be packed with life, always busy. So we got busy with our lives, with recovery. I was absorbed with different things. Not acquiring things, but things that were more important. Basic Jewish values: charity, good things, family. I took care of sick, elderly friends and neighbors, even when I had three small children."

But "I was always there for the children," Lucy says. Her son, Herbert, was her first child; then Ingrid, who later changed her name to Estie (the diminutive of Esther, her Jewish name); and Ronni, the youngest daughter. Caring for her children overshadowed all other obligations.

Most survivors sought to replace the families they had lost in the war. Still others consciously, but many more quite unconsciously, believed that it was only by having children that Hitler's plan to eradicate the Jewish people would ultimately be thwarted, adding a political motivation to their desire to reconstruct their families. Consequently, in larger numbers than other Jewish-Americans at that time, survivors decided to "bring into the world a new generation" (Helmreich, 1992, p. 127).

Concerning the reasons for Lucy's decision to become a full-time homemaker, her personal history—as is true for all survivors—must be added to the mix. When she was a child, Lucy says, "I missed my mother something awful." Lucy's mother had an exhausting, high-pressure job—she was a Jewish woman teaching in a Polish high school, in an era of rampant anti-Semitism. Lucy doesn't fault her for having a career: "My mother did the right thing; she did what she wanted to do. But I missed her. She used to come home in the afternoon and lay down with a headache. She was tired. I was not allowed to wake her. I used to walk into my friends' houses and I envied every one of them. 'My mommy's home,' they would say." Then Lucy moderates her tone, saying: "Whatever minutes my mother had free, she spent with me. But

I definitely made a conscious choice with my three. I would always be there for the children."

Lucy may have always been available, but parenting was not easy for her, particularly when her children were very young. Child survivors who had lost their own parents at a young age, and therefore lost their parenting role models, had an especially difficult time. In addition, when survivors such as Lucy and Jonas married each other, they were deprived of the natural array of generations who offer advice, instruct, or assist with the children: "There was no one to help," Lucy says, "nobody around. There were neighbors, but it was the hardest thing about bringing up the kids, not having any family." Not even those good friends from the Girls Club: "Everyone was busy, or too far away." Lucy says, at first rather plaintively, "I didn't know how to bring up my children." Then she adds: "But I met all challenges."

Jonas was a hard worker and a good provider. He had an uncle who was a butcher, from whom he learned the trade. When his uncle retired, Jonas took over the shop—preparing and selling kosher meat—and he did well. When their son was still a toddler, Lucy and Jonas bought the home in Brooklyn they still live in today, where they began to enjoy a comfortable, middle-class life. When the children were young they spent their summers at bungalow colonies in the Catskills—Fanny's in Ellenville, Sunny Lane in Monticello, Kaplan's in Swan Lake. When the children were old enough to travel, the family spent several summers abroad.

Lucy has made many trips to Israel, sometimes more than once a year, to visit family members who settled there after the war. When Lucy left for America, "Zosia stayed on in Germany until she could go to Israel. She always had a dream to go there." The only one of her mother's four sisters to survive the war, Lucy's Aunt Zosia had witnessed the death of her husband and children in the ghetto. Lucy also had an uncle-in-law who had gone to Israel after the war; he had been married to Lucy's youngest aunt. She and their two children "perished in Auschwitz, but somehow he survived," Lucy says. This uncle and her Aunt Zosia married "after they found one another in Israel." In Judaism there is an ancient law that goes back to the time when Jews practiced polygamy, in which a man was obligated to marry the wife of his deceased brother.[4] The marriage of Lucy's aunt and uncle was not such an obligation, but Lucy thinks of it as having been in the same spirit. And it was a successful marriage; they had a good life together. Not only did they rebuild a large family, with many children and grandchildren, but Zosia also resumed her teaching career. In Lodz, before the war, she taught at a *Beis Yakov*, a Hebrew school for girls; in Israel, she ultimately became a school principal.

Lucy has a strong emotional attachment to the state of Israel: "My grandmother always wanted to go, but then it was a trip by boat of six months." But Israel has a different, more intensely symbolic meaning for survivors. Yael Danieli suggests it is because, in Israel, there is a "mutually reinforcing context of shared mourning, shared memory, a sense that the memory is preserved. . . . a nation that carried the memory [of the Holocaust] as part of its consciousness" (Danieli, 1992, pp. 198–201). Helmreich believes that for many survivors, being in Israel has a cathartic value: "Arabs replaced the Nazis in their demonology and they saw Israel's every victory as a replay of history, in which the Jews emerge victorious over the oppressors" (1992, p. 189). Speaking about her most recent trip to Israel, Lucy confesses: "I always cry when I see *El Al*—our plane—it belongs to us, with a big star on the side."

Lucy's travels with her family have not been limited to Israel. They've been to Egypt and have traveled all over Europe: France, Germany, Spain, and Holland, as well as to Central and Eastern Europe. Although Lucy avoids both reading about the Holocaust and speaking about her own experiences, she did go back to Poland, to her hometown of Lodz—even to Auschwitz. She also returned to Bergen-Belsen with Fran, for the fiftieth anniversary of the liberation. She says: "I buried my mother in Bergen-Belsen. After, when I went there, I wanted to move her body to Israel. I talked to a Rabbi there about it, but he said: 'She is testimony.'"

On the family trips Lucy would introduce her children to the various aspects of secular European culture. But most often, because they were interested in knowing more about Jewish history and culture, the family took tours of Jewish heritage sites. After they moved into their Brooklyn home, Lucy's family had begun attending the "little *shul* just down the street. Lucy sent her children to a parochial school, the Yeshiva of Flatbush. "And slowly," Lucy remembers, "we had become *shomer shabbos*."

Shomer shabbos literally refers to those who observe the Sabbath laws, but is also used to denote those who adhere, generally, to Jewish law. Within Jewish societies worldwide there are varying degrees of religious observance that range from cultural identification with little or no religious observance at one extreme to ultra-Orthodoxy at the other.[5] The Orthodox adhere closely to

Halakha, the collective body of Jewish law that includes the *mitzvot*, or obligations: Talmudic and religious law is based upon interpretation, as well as customs and traditions. This combination of Jewish law and tradition guides not only religious practice and belief but also numerous aspects of day-to-day life.

Over time, the Pasternak family adopted the lifestyle of being observant, Orthodox Jews. It is true that many survivors turned away from Judaism, but studies show that many others, like Lucy's family, retained their identification with Orthodox Judaism. And while survivors, like American Jews, observe Jewish law in varying degrees—the more closely you follow the law, the more observant or "religious" you are—they make up a "disproportional number" of those who identify themselves as Orthodox: 41 percent, in comparison with only about 10 percent of American Jews generally (Helmreich, 1992, p. 79).

There are various reasons that survivors such as Lucy were able to retain their religious beliefs and obligations. "God gave man the freedom to choose. The price of free choice is evil," some said. Further, many insisted that "the Holocaust was perpetrated by man, not God" (Haas, 1996a, p. 144). Lucy defers to her children to explain the Holocaust and accepts their explanation, which basically affirms another commonly expressed rationale, that "finite man cannot understand God's infinite ways." Therefore, man is able to understand neither why the Holocaust occurred nor why some lived and others died. Not incidentally, it's been suggested, such a belief may serve an important, palliative function: "If it was God's decision for you to remain alive, you are relieved of survivor guilt" (Haas, 1996a, p. 152).

Like those survivors who identify themselves as Orthodox Jews, whether or not they are observant, most of the Girls Club women were raised in the Orthodox tradition. For example, even if they did not strictly adhere to the dietary laws (laws of *Kashruth*), most Eastern European Jews carried Jewish traditions based upon Orthodox observance with them to America. They couldn't bring themselves to eat forbidden foods such as pork and shellfish; or they continued to fast on Yom Kippur and go to *shul* on the High Holy Days. There were those, of course, who made a point of shunning traditional practices, but most of the Girls Club women did not lose their faith in God and continue to follow some practices that had been embedded in Polish-Jewish culture.

Lucy believes she did not *become* religious, she progressively became *more* religious: "It was always in me, in my upbringing, which goes way back to two ultra-Orthodox sets of grandparents. My friend Doris remembers at the Girls Club I always said the *Sh'ma* every night, I always prayed." In addition, and very important to Lucy, following an orthodox way of life offers her something that other survivors speak of. It allows them to retain "a sense of continuity through their traditional activities." It helps them to respect their parents' memory. Some say, "I live as they would have wanted me to" (Haas, 1996a, p. 153). Lucy says, "My upbringing by my beloved maternal grandmother left in me deep roots of believing and continuing this spiritual way of life, which I leave for my children and grandchildren to live with." Becoming observant offered Lucy a comprehensive set of guidelines "for living a good and righteous life." If not explicitly, *Halakha* implicitly provided answers to the many unanswered questions she had about bringing up her children.

Holocaust survivors are celebrated for being devoted to their children—to the point of being overprotective, which Lucy admits: "I was fearful for them. I'd say, 'Don't go out at night; don't go out in the dark.' But my daughter would tell me, 'Don't talk that way.' She was right." Lucy's decision not to discuss the Holocaust with her children needs to be seen in this context; it was another effort to protect them. Each survivor had to arrive at a decision about whether or how much to tell their children: "Some parents talked of their experiences and impressed on their children the importance of memory. Others avoided mention of the Holocaust years and attempted, as best they could, to obliterate its influence on their later lives" (Haas, 1996b, p. 9).

Lucy hoped to shield her children from the terrible images she feared would damage their young and tender psyches, from the pain of knowing what their families and parents had suffered, and also from being exposed to her own uncontrolled emotion. "I was afraid I would become hysterical," she admits, "but most of all I thought it was wrong to tell the children. They all say they [survivors' children] are influenced by survivor parents. I didn't want to burden them." Lucy knew that in time her children would learn about the Holocaust: "I thought, they will find out elsewhere." Indeed, they did.

At the children's school, the topic of the Holocaust inevitably came up in their studies of contemporary Jewish history. "One day," Lucy recalls, "my daughter, Ingrid, I found her on the porch. She was crying, hysterical, 'Ma, you didn't tell me.' In the Yeshiva they covered the windows with black cloth and showed pictures of the Holocaust."

Despite her lack of openness with them, perhaps because of it, Lucy realizes that her children were unavoidably and inevitably affected by the Holocaust. Negatively in some ways, but also positively: "My values are in part a result of the Holocaust, and so the Holocaust also affected their values and their achievement; but not only the Holocaust. My values were established before the war, in my family. Many in my family were educated. We had especially independent women. But it's known that survivors gave them the foundation and pushed their children to be successful."

While she is essentially a humble person, Lucy can't help but take pride in her children's considerable achievements: Lucy's son is a doctor, the cliché of a Jewish mother's dream come true; one of her daughters is a social worker; the other is a special education teacher. They are all Orthodox; her daughter, Ronni, is ultra-Orthodox. Her daughters, in addition to earning their degrees and pursuing careers, have solid marriages, and Lucy has many grandchildren. (She wouldn't say how many, fearful of being too boastful—of the "evil eye?" And then laughs at herself.)[6] Some of Lucy's friends told me they are envious of her, which also makes her very uncomfortable (and is rooted in the same superstition, fear of those, Lucy says, "who might not *fagin* [who begrudge] you").

Lucy has a single regret: "I come from a very educated family, what happened to me?" she plaintively asks. Although she continued to educate herself informally, Lucy's greatest disappointment is that she never earned her degree. A few years ago, when we first met, she confides: "My son begged me until today, please go back to college. But I had three little kids. And when they grew up and got married, then I started to babysit for my grandchildren. So I never had time to go back. I regret that, very much so. But one woman I know became a doctor of chemistry. She was busy with her Ph.D. and when her son needed her, she wasn't there. She has a very guilty conscience."

Finally, Lucy concludes: "I do feel badly that I never went back to school, but I don't feel guilty staying with my children and my grandchildren. If you didn't do it, you can never make it up."

Lucy's friend Betty (Lucy still calls her Bronka) was actually the first of the two to marry. Betty had been living at the Girls Club for more than three years when she met Hy Berman at a concert at Lewisohn Stadium. They've been married now for sixty years. The wedding took place in March 1950 at Temple Emanuel in Brooklyn, and the reception was held at the Girls Club. Rose Feldman, the administrator of the Girls Club Betty remembers as "that kind, loving woman," and Rose's husband, stood in place of Betty's parents. In one of Betty's wedding photos, Lucy and Betty have their arms entwined: Lucy, looks slim, youthful, happy; Betty is beaming, impish, her eyes twinkle. In fact, they still do.

However much was similar about their early years, Betty's adult life took a very different path from Lucy's. When she and Hy married, she had a "decent job," Betty says, working as a secretary at the Federation of Jewish Philanthropies. Hy, the Brooklyn-born son of a garment worker, was enrolled in a Ph.D. program in American labor history at Columbia University. Unlike Lucy, Betty continued to work for the next eight years—until she had the first of her two children. By the time Hy completed his doctorate and secured a teaching post at Brooklyn College, they were living in a "wonderful, rent-controlled apartment on Riverside Drive."

Betty had dropped out of high school to attend business school. But she'd later earned an equivalency diploma and began attending Hunter College, part-time—until 1960. Hy was offered a faculty position at Michigan State University, and then, only a year later, at the University of Minnesota in Minneapolis. Betty's last job in New York was in the history department at Columbia, as secretary to Salo Baron, a Jewish historian recognized as one of the great scholars of his time for his sweeping opus, A Social and Religious History of the Jews. Betty worked for him during the preparation of one of the manuscripts (and was honored to have been mentioned in the acknowledgments for her contribution to the work).[7]

During the time that Betty lived in Manhattan, she tried to keep in touch with Lucy. But Betty visited her only once. She thinks it was because Lucy was totally involved with homemaking and parenting; "she was always busy." But that may not have been the only reason they drifted apart. While they had a strong bond of affection, their lives were taking such different directions that the young women no longer had very much in common. However, Betty did maintain her friendship with Fran who had moved to Long Island. Fran's husband, Seymour Berlin, ran a successful printing business he had taken over from his father. Over time, after she moved to Minneapolis, Betty lost touch with most of her friends in New York—except for Alex, a man she'd developed a close friendship with in the DP camp at Zeilsheim; and Fran, the one friend from the Girls Club with whom she has kept in touch throughout the years.

Betty had become very close to Hy's parents, who lived in the New York area. When they lived in Manhattan, Betty felt she was part of a family again. But when she and Hy moved to Minneapolis, Betty says, with two young children and no family or old friends nearby, life at first was difficult for her. Although she was married to an American, she believes it was as difficult for her as it had been for Lucy. She missed her in-laws but, in addition, had to adjust to an unfamiliar, non-Jewish, midwestern culture that had been heavily influenced by the early Scandinavian settlers. Adding to her feeling of disconnection from her new surroundings, Betty didn't know any other survivors in the area. She joined the Reform Temple, but didn't find her community there. "I've always had a conflict with Judaism," Betty confided. Unlike Lucy, but like other survivors whose religious beliefs "were weakened, if not destroyed" by the Holocaust (Suedfeld, 2002, p. 17), Betty says, "God was looking the other way."

Still, Betty was determined to cope, to make the adjustment to yet another major change in her life and to move on. And she was happy in her new city. For a European and a former New Yorker, even in the 1960s, Minneapolis had all the features and amenities of a great cosmopolitan city. Both Minneapolis and St. Paul, its sister city on the other side of the Mississippi River, are urbane and sophisticated.[8]

Betty and Hy made many friends in Minneapolis. When they arrived they were made to feel welcome; they were invited to meet other faculty at college functions. They were invited to dinner parties and other social events, although Betty remembers experiencing these initial meetings "with trepidation; and what's more, I had to reciprocate." Betty was very insecure as the young wife of an intellectual, having to deal with other academics: "I lacked confidence in academic settings. I felt uneducated, inarticulate, unworthy." It was an emotional throwback: "I'd felt the same way as I did at the Girls Club. I felt like an outsider, since I didn't go to college."

Betty settled into her new life, in a place she learned to love, in a house she loved (and still does, after more than forty-five years). She and Hy went to concerts and to the theater with their new friends. They became familiar with the city's many diverse ethnic neighborhoods. Her children were enrolled in

St. Paul Academy, a private school with a good reputation. Betty could finally begin to think about what more she wanted. "It was time," she decided, "to return to school."

Betty believes her decision was clearly "affected by feminism," that is, by the revival of the feminist movement that had begun about ten years before, in the early 1960s; she was excited by changes she was beginning to notice. She began to reconsider whether the opportunity for her to complete her degree had passed. "Even though I didn't do it at the right time, when I should have, when I was younger," Betty says, she came to realize it wasn't too late. Some professions, such as law and medicine, were beginning to attract many more women. Academic programs were beginning to address the special needs of mature women like Betty. They came to be known as "returning women," applying to colleges in ever-increasing numbers to complete their degrees after absences of many years.

In New York, Betty had taken some courses at Hunter College and Columbia University; now she enrolled at the University of Minnesota. In time, she was awarded a bachelor of arts degree in art history through the Metropolitan State College in Minneapolis, an alternative program that accepted and combined all of her credits. It was an outstanding achievement for a woman of her background and generation, one she'd deeply desired since she was a young girl.

Betty loved art history and it would always be important to her, but she was not going to have a career as an art historian. She loved books as much, or more. "I always wanted to be a librarian," Betty told me. From the time she had been a little girl in Lodz she was an avid reader; the first book she remembers was *Little Women*. I asked, "Why that book?" But I didn't expect her answer: "It was the first book on the list because of the author's name; Louisa Alcott began with an A." Betty continued to read even in the ghetto while she was still able to get books from the library; she remembers reading *Gone with the Wind* and some Dostoyevsky. Again I was surprised at her choices until she corrected my assumption. It wasn't a matter of choice at all: "There was no children's literature as we understand it, I read whatever they had."

When Betty was studying for her art history degree she'd taken some library courses, but then the university closed its library school. The closest school was out of the question; it was in Illinois. However, the university did continue to offer some off-campus courses in library science. After Betty got her first library job as an aide, she traveled to towns where the courses were offered so that she could put herself in line for a higher position. Although she never earned her degree, she took so many courses that she has the equivalent of a master's degree in library science.

When the children were still young, Betty was happy to have a part-time job. But when an opening for a job as an assistant librarian arose, the timing was right for her to apply for full-time work, and at a higher level. She was offered a job as the administrator of a storefront library in a Polish neighborhood in northeast Minneapolis, "because I knew the language," Betty says. While the population by then was mostly second generation Polish-Americans, a good number of the first generation, who had emigrated earlier in the century, still lived there.

"I loved it," Betty says. Because she didn't have the degree she couldn't be designated head librarian, but she was, in fact, in charge of the library. She developed and organized programs, went into schools and did a great deal of outreach, and as her accomplishments became apparent, Betty developed confidence in herself. "They threatened to close the library several times because it was so small," she says. But with her newfound self-assurance, she organized protests that kept the library open for another six or seven years, until it was relocated to a beautiful newly renovated building in the huge old Grain Belt Brewery. The library, renamed for one of the most colorful characters in early local history, Pierre Bottineau, has thrived in its new location.[9] But by that time, Betty was ready for a "new challenge." She transferred to a library in East Lake, close to home. There, she turned her attention to an area of library science that was new to her and built an impressive reference collection. It wasn't until 2006, after more than thirty years of working in the library system, that Betty finally retired.

Being a librarian, Betty says, was "a transformative experience." She had achieved success, status, and the self-confidence she'd never had before. "Even those without such disadvantages didn't have such a career. But my career as a librarian was successful by any standard," Betty says, justifiably proud of what she'd accomplished—for her community as well as for herself. As one researcher pointed out about child survivors such as Betty, success in their occupations was "not a negligible achievement for people whose past was so disrupted and whose future was predicted to be so bleak" (Suedfeld, 2002, p. 14). Nor was her successful career Betty's only achievement. Although she never pursued a career as an art historian, Betty's love of art and art history remained an essential part of her life.

In 1975, Betty began a two-year training program as a docent at the Minneapolis Institute of Arts. She was an anomaly among the cadre of docents, since that role is usually the purview of the ladies of the Junior League and the upper-crust of Minneapolis society. But Betty was never put off; in fact, she's been leading tours there ever since. Betty became an expert in Asian art, particularly Chinese and more recently Japanese art, giving tours of the Institute's relatively small but internationally renowned collection. I was fortunate, when I visited her in Minneapolis, to have had the pleasure of a private tour; Betty's knowledge is so deep and vast, and she knows her subject so well and is so comfortable with the details, that there is nothing in the least pretentious or pedantic about her presentation.

Betty's easy manner as a docent has surely been enhanced by her extensive travels in Asia, particularly her lengthy stays in China, which she has visited four times. Her first trip, to Tianjin, was in 1981. Betty explains: "China was just then beginning to open to the West. Hy, a labor historian interested in political radicalism, was invited to teach a course for Chinese history teachers at Nankai University, about sixty miles from Beijing. He was the first American historian to go there at that time." As a result, Betty was able to spend five months studying Chinese art and reading Chinese history. In addition, while in China she was asked to lecture to teachers and librarians about the American library system. The Chinese government arranged for her to travel to many parts of the country, and provided a guide and translator. Betty and Hy were able to make several other, shorter trips to China when, after their initial visit, many Chinese students came to study at the University of Minnesota (the first university in the country to develop a program with China, which lasted over a five-year period).

Betty had opportunities to study European art as well, when Hy taught American history in Munich during a summer program there, and again in Amsterdam. While she was in the Netherlands she wrote a guide to Dutch museums for a course she was enrolled in at the University of Minnesota, and for which she earned credits that were applied to her bachelor's degree. Hy and Betty also traveled extensively throughout the United States (they spent an academic year at Berkeley), in Europe, and in Israel, sometimes accompanied by one or both of their children.

Betty's beloved Aunt Genia lived in Israel until her death in 1970. Betty was always in close correspondence with her and visited her several times. Although she regrets that she could not be there "at the end," Betty is grateful that her aunt had a good life in Israel. Not only was Genia happily married, she had a career as a children's clothing designer. While Betty still believes that emigrating to America "was the right decision," for her, like Lucy and many other survivors, she has a very strong emotional attachment to Israel. "It is my identity," she says. Because Betty is a fierce defender of Israel's right to exist, she confesses that she tends to have negative attitudes toward Muslims—an anomaly in her otherwise liberal worldview and one that she struggles against.

Betty never returned to Poland during any of her European travels. Not that she avoids reminders of the Holocaust or denies her own history. She did eventually make contact with the community of Holocaust survivors in the Twin Cities area and sees them on such occasions as the annual Holocaust memorial ceremony. Although she's the youngest of the group, and none live nearby, they have a cordial relationship. Unlike Lucy, as her children were growing up Betty did tell them about her Holocaust experiences, discussing what she felt was "appropriate for them to understand at different ages and times." She made it her "conscious policy not to bring it up, but tried to respond honestly whenever it did come up." Betty believes: "It would have been intellectually dishonest to do otherwise. How could I pretend it didn't happen?" And, she says, "I felt that the children had to know, I wanted them to understand the authentic experience. I thought it would make better people of them." Betty will also talk about her personal history with friends if it comes up in conversation. But she never brings up the topic: "I don't live my life that way. I wanted to be normal. I didn't want people to feel sorry for me."

Betty doesn't seek out reminders of the Holocaust: she doesn't need to. She says, echoing Lucy's sentiments: "Survivor is close to the top of my list when it comes to my identity." In this they are, with all of their significant differences, still very much alike. And the two women are similar in some other respects as well: They've traveled widely but have also lived comfortably within their communities. Both women have had good, long marriages. As with Lucy, Betty's grown children are professionals. Her daughter, Ruth Berman, is an editor and writes children's books; Ruth has a daughter of her own, Betty's much-loved grandchild. Betty's son, Steven, is doing postdoctoral work in plant genetics. But the chief similarity is that both women are satisfied with the life choices they made.

Now Betty and Lucy, indeed all of the women who lived at the Girls Club with them, have most of their years behind them. The following and final chapter in these life stories is a closer look at the issues they and other elderly "child" survivors are facing today.

NOTES

1. See Haas's discussion which begins on p. 9 of *In the Shadow of the Holocaust*. He speaks from his personal experience as well as from his research.

2. As, indeed, Suedfeld does, perhaps inadvertently, in *Life from the Ashes: Social Science Careers of Young Holocaust Refugees and Survivors*.

3. For additional references, as well as my own elaborated discussion of these issues, see Ford, *The Girls*.

4. It is known as the Levirite marriage. The most positive explanation is that it was incumbent upon the brother to assume care and support of his brother's family. But it also served the purpose of keeping his brother's estate in the family.

5. The other major Jewish sects are Reform, Conservative, and Reconstructionist.

6. The evil eye (a malignant spiritual influence caused by the jealousy of others) has historically been a popular superstition among Jews.

7. Some consider Salo Baron (1895–1989) the greatest Jewish historian of the twentieth century. After teaching at the Jewish Teachers College in Vienna in 1926, he was invited by Rabbi Stephen S. Wise to teach at the Jewish Institute of Religion in New York. He began his career at Columbia in the newly established Miller Chair of Jewish History, Literature, and Institutions in 1930.

8. St. Paul has a bit of an inferiority complex since it's dominated by the richer cultural life of its bigger sister. First, there is the University of Minnesota sitting along the banks of the river, with all it has to offer, including its Weisman Art Museum housed in a spectacular Frank Gehry structure. And there are other museums: the American Swedish Institute, the Museum of Russian Art, the Minneapolis Institute of Arts, the Minnesota Historical Society. The Tyrone Guthrie theater complex rivals the Gehry building for visual ingenuity and innovation. Minneapolis's many diverse ethnic neighborhoods have shops and restaurants

typical of such neighborhoods. Moreover, compared with New York City, they are all within an easily negotiated area.

9. Pierre Bottineau (1817–1895) was an accomplished guide, trapper, and trader. He spent the prime years of his long, active life opening up the Northwest Corridor communities of the Twin Cities metro area to settlement. As to the brewery, Minneapolis has many now-abandoned breweries that have been transformed into useful, active spaces.

Child Survivors in Old Age

The Aging Women

Life is a struggle, yes, it's not easy, but you have to learn to live with it, to make the best of it.

—*Doris (Dorka Izbicka) Wasserman*

"It was the greatest thing that happened to me. I got away from widows," Fran says about the Girls Club. She is referring to the period before she moved in, when she rented rooms from widowed women. Recently, after having nursed her husband through a long and difficult illness, Fran became a widow herself. She is now coping with one of the most difficult ordeals that can confront an aging woman. Among the women of the Girls Club, only Betty (Basia) has been widowed for some time. The others still face this life-altering event, along with the other daunting challenges presented by old age,

As discussed in the previous chapter, the women have had many parallel experiences throughout their lives, to which each reacted in her own unique way. The same can be said for the ways in which they are dealing with the difficulties of aging. Aging, a singular process for each individual, involves a broad range of experiences and is affected by genetics and physical condition, environment and lifestyle choices, personality, and many other factors. Yet there are inescapable similarities among the women of the Girls Club, all of whom are approaching or are now in their eighties. Overall, they are aging well. In spite of a formidable list of negative age-related challenges that contemporary researchers have identified, gerontologists are frequently surprised by how well many people cope—and even more surprised by how well many Holocaust survivors, such as the Girls Club women, are managing.[1]

But it is important not to oversimplify, advises Yael Danieli. As important as external markers of success—such as professional or business accomplishments, or close and loving families—are, they can also mask hidden problems: "Survivors have areas of [both] vulnerability and resilience." Danieli warns against drawing conclusions "based on outward appearances" alone, particularly with elderly survivors, who are often reluctant to talk about their concerns or to seek help from counselors or psychologists.[2]

In order to understand how the women are dealing with the many potential obstacles to successful aging (and keeping Danieli's cautions in mind), it's worth examining some of the major issues and problems related to the aging process that, we now know, may affect aging Holocaust survivors differently from others. It will be useful to look at what studies of aging have shown, and what some of the many researchers in the field of gerontology are saying.

Gerontology is a relatively new field, a multidisciplinary study of the social-psychological and physical aspects of aging. It wasn't until 1945 that the founders of the Gerontological Society of America began to view the processes of aging as a legitimate area of study and research.[3] (It is completely separate from geriatrics, which is a branch of medicine that specializes in diseases of the elderly.) Initially, until it broadened its approach, gerontology's focus was on the physical and psychological processes of decline.

Today the elderly population continues to grow. Because people live longer and healthier lives, the oldest of the old, those eighty-five and older, could make up a quarter of the population in coming years (Society and Aging, 2009, p. 5).[4] As a result, the body of accumulated knowledge related to gerontology has become increasingly prominent and is helpful in understanding many aspects of aging in our society (and in some other Western societies, although generalizations must be made with caution since there are genetic and cultural differences that must be taken into account).

Wide-ranging studies continue to examine normal aging and age-related problems, the effects of the aging population on society, and the needs of the elderly. Some studies are very narrowly focused. For example, a recent study looked at the high incidence of falls among the elderly and their often fatal consequences. Once dismissed as an inevitable result of changes in mobility, falls are now being appreciated as complex events that may be prevented (Leland, 2008, p. A1). Another study focuses on whether and how stress accelerates the aging process (Stein, 2004, p. A1).[5] As a result of such research, some widely-held conclusions now exist about what happens as the body and mind age.

Many changes that accompany aging are experienced by even the healthiest individuals. Although the list is formidable, these processes are normal and are not necessarily debilitating. They include various sensory changes, such as diminished vision and hearing, as well as decreases in flexibility and strength, speed of response and execution, fine-motor control and hand-eye coordination. In addition, degenerative diseases such as arthritis, rheumatism, and osteoporosis may affect agility and mobility. Changes in memory, reasoning, and abstract thinking are also common. Processing information may take a little longer.

Social changes related to aging, particularly for women, may include adjusting to decreased income and earning capacity. The elderly may also experience the loss of social and familial ties after retiring and moving to a new home. Things that were never an issue, such as access to transportation, may become a problem for those who no longer drive (or for those, most often women, who never learned to drive). All of these circumstances can lead to changes in social activity that may bring along with them feelings of loneliness, stress, anxiety about becoming dependent on others, and fears about safety and security. And there are the major, seismic changes that occur with the death of a spouse, such as the ones Fran is now experiencing.

Largely as a result of the women's movement, with its focus on gender studies, a subcategory of gerontology has begun to emerge in recent years. While men and women deal with many similar issues, some have come to be thought of as women's or men's issues depending upon which sex is "more likely to experience them" (Hatch, 2000, p. 175). (It is the same distinction, incidentally, that has been made in Holocaust studies, and doesn't mean that either is sex is more or less successful in dealing with them.) It has been found that, because women live longer than men and because it is usual to marry a man who is older, women are more likely to experience the loss of a spouse (a "woman's" issue), resulting not only in extreme stress but also, for some, poverty in old age (another "woman's" issue, but fortunately not one for the women in this life history). But widowers also suffer greatly from the loss of a spouse. Men often depend on their wives as their sole intimate confidante—many mourn the loss of their "best friend" (a "man's" issue); women generally have a network of close friends and relationships that can help them through this critical time. Until recently, retirement was seen as a man's issue. And it is known that women and men face different health issues—women more commonly must cope with chronic illness and depression.[6]

In addition to the normal changes that occur with aging, elderly Holocaust survivors may face particular problems. And today *all* survivors are elderly; the women of the Girls Club were twelve to fifteen years old when the war ended in 1945, but most survivors were older, between fifteen and thirty-five. Even the youngest, a child who was born at the very end of the war, will be sixty-five in 2010, while the oldest survivors are in their nineties. As they faced special difficulties in the postwar years, when they were still coping with post-traumatic stresses, some Holocaust survivors now find the process of aging more difficult than it is for the general population. For many reasons, survivors may be distinctly vulnerable to psychological stresses that affect all elderly.

Feelings of loneliness and dependence or concerns about safety or security are uncomfortably familiar for Holocaust survivors. Those who were totally absorbed in the hard work of rebuilding their lives and caring for their new families, who never had the time for other interests or diversions, may have particular difficulty finding satisfying substitutes for their work when they retire. Their free and unstructured days may allow too much time for unhealthy reflection over their losses, including the loss of their childhoods.[7] "Worrying about the potential need for residential care or actual entry into a nursing home is especially difficult for survivors. This is not their first experience with the loss of home, family, community, privacy and freedom"; while moving to an institutional setting is distressful for anyone, for survivors it can be "reminiscent of early life losses" (David & Pelly, 2003, p. 20). Survivors who suffered massive losses during the Holocaust may reexperience their earlier sorrow in response to the death of friends or relatives. At the thought of losing their spouse, the fear of "abandonment threatens them anew" (Kestenberg & Kahn, 1998, p. 156).

Most survivors never had the opportunity to witness the healthy aging of parents or grandparents because these family members perished during the

war. In the camps, young people saw the sick, handicapped, and elderly immediately murdered. In the ghettos, the elderly were the first to be deported,
if they hadn't already succumbed to disease or famine. After the war, if survivors married other survivors, which most did, there was no opportunity to
observe in-laws or extended family members going through the normal aging
processes. For most survivors, therefore, aging inevitably represents frailty
and vulnerability, weakness and decline.

In addition, when they lose a loved one, aging survivors of the Holocaust
may actually be grieving long-standing and massive losses for the first time.
They may never have gone through the psychological stages of mourning
that can result in accepting death. Leo Eitinger, a psychiatrist and Holocaust
survivor who had extensive clinical contact with many concentration camp
survivors after the war, was one of the first to write about their failure to engage in the grieving process, the necessary mourning period that accompanies
loss. He wrote that some were too ill or too traumatized to grieve: "During
the war, they had been unable to afford the luxury of that letdown—after the
war they faced the pressures of adapting to a new country, new language, new
customs, and new responsibilities" (1993, p. 10).

Survivors were never able to experience the ritualized grieving process
which, for Jews, involves the funeral service and rituals related to interment.
Most of those killed were buried in mass graves or burned in the ovens of
the death camps. Yael Danieli quotes a survivor who asks: "'How does one
bury smoke? How does one place headstones in the sky? How does one
bring flowers to the clouds?'" (1992, p. 196). Danieli says that these words
illustrate only a few of the numerous obstacles that survivors face in their
attempt to mourn and subsequently to heal. Nor were survivors able to
engage in Jewish rituals related to the week-long, post-funeral commemora-
tion called *shiva* during which, in normal times, friends and family come to
the home to reminisce and to grieve together, and to bring food, nourishment, to the bereaved. As a result, for survivors, feelings of grief from recent
losses may be compounded by those from long ago, making their sense of
loss multifaceted, highlighting past traumas and magnifying feelings of
loneliness and isolation.

Much has been written about "triggers," circumstances that may evoke
painful memories for the Holocaust survivor. These may include everyday
activities—undressing or removing jewelry, entering a darkened room, using

a public toilet, even eating a certain food.[8] Activities that occur in a medical facility or hospital may have particular meaning for a Holocaust survivor—taking a shower, being confined in a small space, dealing with crowded conditions, shaving or hair cutting, receiving injections, lining up for treatment, the sudden beam of a flashlight, or illness and weakness itself.[9] When triggers occur, they take the survivor back to an event as if it were happening at that moment. Lucy told me that she once saw a woman wearing a scarf that, for that moment, took her back to the ghetto. "Memory," as the writer Elizabeth Rosner points out, "means that you can be in two places at the same time."[10] For Holocaust survivors, memories are never far below the surface: they intrude easily.

A *palimpsest* is defined as a manuscript, typically of papyrus or parchment, in which new text has been written over the earlier version, sometimes more than once, and in which the earlier writing is legible. Sometimes the earlier writing bleeds through despite layer upon layer of new script. For many elderly survivors, memories of the Holocaust, like a palimpsest, seep through despite layer upon layer of experiences—a lifetime of layers—that might have obscured the earlier ones. For a survivor the Holocaust is, literally, the experience of a lifetime. Its aftereffects extend into old age, no matter how successful are the coping strategies and mechanisms that enable the individual to lead a relatively normal life. The extraordinary thing, however, is not that the Holocaust is always there—how could it not be? It is, instead, that, despite dire predictions to the contrary, survivors have been able to develop effective coping skills.

Notably, child survivors have shown extraordinary resilience, an "ability to overcome the odds, or make markedly successful adaptations" (Greene, 2005, p. 2). The early literature on Holocaust survivors, and intuition, told us that wouldn't happen. Child survivors were thought to have been traumatized beyond repair, their normal development effectively compromised. "How is it possible not to become completely mad after such a personal and collective disaster?" asks Aaron Haas, a writer whose parents were survivors. Yet, he continues, "While survivors experience inordinate vulnerability, or death anxiety, or ongoing fears of losing those dearest to them, what is truly remarkable is the fact that they are not paralyzed by their apprehensions" (1996a, p. 68); it is truly remarkable that so many child survivors, such as the women whose psychological repair began in the Girls Club, went on to lead relatively healthy lives.

As we know, the early literature on Holocaust survivors had been mainly drawn from clinical studies that were heavily focused on those who found it difficult or were unable to cope. For forty-five years after the Holocaust came to an end, little was known about those individuals, including child survivors, who were dealing successfully with the challenges inherent in building new lives. Dr. Esther Greenglass, an expert in the field of aging survivors, says about the first North American studies (published in 1990) of a nonclinical population that examined how elderly survivors coped and adjusted: "Their results showed that most of them suffered after the war and were still suffering from the effects of persecution. Despite their mental suffering, however, they managed to cope and to adjust. They were successful in work and society and they managed to raise warm families" (2002, p. 2).[11]

The studies that Dr. Greenglass refers to, and others that have been cited previously, support the view that these survivors, although they may bear the scars of their earlier trauma, are continuing their positive adjustment into old age.[12] They are coping by dealing effectively with physical decline. Those who attend to elderly people's physical well-being find that disabilities and chronic illnesses, "once thought to be inseparable from aging," are no longer inevitable: "This view is rapidly changing as the means are developed to prevent, treat or control diseases" (Subgoal 1, 2001, p. 1).

Survivors are also, for the most part, making the necessary psychological and social adjustments that enable successful adult development to continue in old age. At one time, major personality theorists completely ignored adulthood, and certainly aging, as a significant period of development (Freud and Piaget, for example). We now know that human psychological and social development continues throughout life. Erik Erikson was the first to expand his theory of the stages of human development into adulthood. Although he formulated his ideas more than fifty years ago, and despite the fact that some of his assertions have faced intense criticism, he remains the prime reference for those who try to define what it means to age well psychologically. Erikson's ideas are helpful in understanding the difference between those who can and those who cannot master the stresses and everyday demands of old age.

Erikson says that at each stage in human development there is a conflict, which he refers to as a crisis, that must be resolved. In the period he
called late adulthood (that is, old age) the most important psychological
challenge is to look back upon your life and come to accept it in a positive
way.[13] This is an extremely difficult task for elderly Holocaust survivors
who, as they reflect upon their lives, may be unable to move beyond their
anger and frustration because "the destruction was unjust, *senseless*" (Haas,
1996a, p. 42). Many survivors are still trying to understand why they were
caught up in an episode in human history that continues to confound even
the most brilliant experts in the field of Holocaust studies. Yet, Erikson
proposes, acceptance is necessary since the alternative is to fall into a state
of despair. And acceptance is possible; many, despite extreme trauma and
great tragedy in their lives, have come to look back on their lives with
contentment.

Some theorists have gone further than Erikson and suggest that it is even
possible to find benefit amid trauma: "that finding benefit in trauma may
reduce later stress; it seems to permit resolution of the experience, allowing
the person to move forward with life" (Greenglass, 2002, p. 3). Think of those
who have lost someone to an illness or problem that is little understood or
underfunded, and who then devote themselves to publicizing the issue or to
raising money for research. There are many examples; for one, the organization known as Mothers Against Drunk Driving (MADD) was founded by
a Texas mother after her thirteen-year-old daughter was killed by a drunk
driver. For such people, these actions can give meaning to the death of their
loved one. Many Holocaust survivors have become involved in educational
and other programs for this very reason. They have given testimony to such
organizations as Steven Spielberg's Righteous Persons Foundation or the
United States Holocaust Memorial Museum, or they have written their memoirs. Some survivors, such as Nobel Laureate Elie Wiesel, have achieved great
stature and are world renowned.

Miles Lerman (who, coincidentally, was related to a Girls Club resident)
became a founding father of the United States Holocaust Memorial Museum.
He led the nationwide campaign to raise money to build the museum, helped
establish its permanent exhibition and build its extensive archives, and served
as the museum's first chairman. Lerman, who was well-known as a partisan
leader in Poland during the war, also helped established the Miles Lerman

Center for the Study of Jewish Resistance to dispel the myth that Jews did not resist the Nazis.

Such activities recall the early, post–World War II writings of Viktor Frankl, a well-known psychologist and Auschwitz survivor.[14] He wrote that growth and emotional maturity can result from turning suffering into achievement and accomplishment, from drawing upon it to change oneself for the better. What's more, Frankl believed that we need to learn to accept our inability to fully comprehend the ultimate meaning of every experience. Frankl and others (like Lucy) found this capacity in religious faith. Others, like Betty (Basia), found meaning in the belief that she was spared "for a purpose." Sadly, those who cannot resist dwelling upon the pain, loss, horrors, and injustice of their early years, who cannot find a counterweight when they look back upon their lives as a whole, may descend into despair.

One helpful, common sense source for information about successful aging is Dr. George Vaillant, director of one of the longest studies of aging ever conducted in the United States: the Study of Adult Development at Harvard University. The project has followed the lives of three diverse groups (a total of 824 people) who were selected as teenagers in 1938. Drawing upon data accumulated from records that have been kept over a sixty-year period, Vaillant finds that those who have aged well—that is, those who demonstrate physical and mental well-being—have a number of things in common. They keep themselves as physically fit as they can, but even some who were ill did not define themselves as "sick" (2002, p. 203). There is a difference, Vaillant writes, between objective and subjective health; that is, between having an illness but not "feeling sick when you get out of bed to face the day" (2002, p. 187), a difference that is reflected in attitude. Looking at yourself in "very old age," Vaillant continues, "is like the inspection of an old, old tree. One can mourn the branches pruned by time that no longer are or one can admire the craggy simplicity that remains" (2002, p. 159).

Vaillant identified additional characteristics among those in the Harvard study who, by his definition, have aged well. Like the women of the Girls Club, the well-adjusted have been in long and stable marriages. Also, in their retirement years they found new and enjoyable activities; they've replaced workmates with new friends and acquaintances. Some have found creative outlets for their energy; some have continued their lifelong learning (Vaillant, 2002, p. 225). Most important, they have developed what he refers to as "mature defenses" so that, when they inspect their "old tree," they are satisfied that their lives still have meaning and dignity (Vaillant, 2002, p. 62).

Mature defenses include the ability to put things in perspective, to laugh at yourself, to step outside yourself even if it means becoming, at times, what Lucy describes as "curiously detached." Mature defenses involve not taking everything too seriously and being flexible, optimistic, and future oriented (2002, p. 305). It would seem that these personality characteristics are innate, that in old age it is too late to practice or learn such new attitudes. But while temperament is important, and may have a basis in genetics, "our genes are not set in plaster," Vaillant explains. "It is also our genes that are programmed to permit us to grow and to change" (2002, p. 305).

Holocaust survivors, such as the women of the Girls Club, confirm Vaillant's conclusion: Adverse experiences do not necessarily lead to permanent damage to the personality. The women of the Girls Club whose stories are told here are aging well. That is not to say that their lives are problem-free, that they never have their moments of despair. But they illustrate many of the characteristics of those in the Harvard study who are coping successfully with the stresses of aging. Here is a brief review of each of the women's stories, and a look at what is happening in their lives today:

Irma (Stermer) Sangiamo. None of the women define themselves as sick—not even Irma, who has suffered from a serious disability, normal pressure hydrocephalus, that was first diagnosed in 1993. She has suffered severe hearing loss, some recent problems with her vision, and has had several episodes of complications from her condition. These include some short-term memory loss (although her long-term memory is amazing, particularly for details). One setback, which occurred in 2000, required four brain operations. Then, in 2004, Irma suffered a serious fall that forced her to retire from her career as a librarian, albeit reluctantly, at the age of seventy-five. When Irma talks about her life since her retirement, you don't hear the voice of a sick person:

> So far I haven't undertaken any outside work of any kind. Silly as it sounds, I don't have time. I do more housework than I did while I was working. I've joined Weight Watchers-on-line and, since my husband's quadruple artery bypass made all my cholesterol-filled cooking methods out of bounds, I have

redeveloped an interest in cooking which I hadn't had. Now we eat from new, healthful recipes every day.

I have photographs from thirty years back waiting to be organized. I have manuals for all sorts of electronic equipment waiting to be studied. I have needlepoint patterns which I'd been saving "for my retirement," waiting to be worked on—and I can't imagine where I ever found thirty-five hours a week for going to work.

Despite her disabilities, Irma is happy with the life choices she made. She's had a very happy marriage. The only one of the European women in the Girls Club to marry a non-Jew, Irma was embraced by her husband Abby's large and warm Italian family. She lived a contented middle-class life. Like Betty (Bronka), Irma was a faculty wife who had her own career (and also was a librarian). Her children are successful professionals. She enjoys her grandchildren. She has many friends, some from work with whom she still meets, periodically, for lunch.

Irma, whose parents sent her from Austria to safety in a children's home in France, from which she was taken to the United States, doesn't think of herself as a Holocaust survivor. She said that she used to be embarrassed when someone referred to her that way since she felt that, compared with the Polish girls, her "experiences were a piece of cake." Nevertheless, like the Polish girls, she lost her home and almost all of her family in the war. Her father survived by escaping to Palestine, but Irma never saw him again.

Yet Irma is not embittered, and is not spending her remaining precious years mourning her losses. Rather, she is looking forward to the future and to her husband's planned retirement from his teaching duties at the Maryland Institute College of Art. By that time she may have finally completed all of those tasks waiting to be done.

I contacted Irma recently, concerned that she might not be well, since she hadn't responded to a card I'd sent. She laughed at herself: "You know, I meant to. Sometimes I think I've done something when I've only thought about doing it. But hey! I'm almost eighty years old."

Betty (Basia Pasternak) Ratchik. Betty is the youngest of the group, only seven years old when the war began. As a result, she shows more of the lasting effects of trauma that are thought to affect child survivors. For one thing, her memories of the war and the period immediately afterward are very sketchy.

I was able to piece together some of her history from a wartime diary and memoir written by Betty's brother, Jonas (Lucy's husband). Betty, who has been a widow for well over a decade, is now able to reflect upon her life with a sense of satisfaction; she doesn't doubt that she's done her best.

Betty suffered extreme trauma as a child: she lost her parents and went into hiding in a cellar, which she describes as not much more than a dark hole in the ground. After the war, she wandered with Jonas and her older sister, from her homeland in Galicia through Eastern Europe. They finally settled in Bad Wiesenthal, a town on the German-Austrian border that was formerly a spa; private homes and hotels had been converted to accommodate refugees. They remained there for a long time—four years—before they came to America.

When Betty moved to the Girls Club, it was because her social workers at the Jewish Federation thought it would be a good placement for her. She graduated from Seward Park High School and would have liked to study nursing but never continued her education, a decision she still regrets. Curiously, she thinks it was because she identified learning and education with Germans.

Betty was content to live at the Girls Club but, other than developing a friendship with Renee, she remained mostly uninvolved; she says, "I went through the motions." Her detachment (a characteristic that researchers say is common among young survivors of extreme trauma) is a pattern that has remained consistent throughout her life, Betty says; she has friends in the retirement community in New Jersey where she has lived since her husband retired, but her intimate relationships are exclusively with her family. She is close to her two daughters and to her grandchildren: "My daughter who lives nearby picks me up and I spend the weekends there. Or sometimes with my other daughter who lives in New City."

While she has been content in the traditional role of homemaker, mother, and grandmother, Betty's most joyous times are bittersweet. Even after all these years she longs to share such moments—her daughters' weddings, her grandchildren's Bar and Bat Mitzvot—with those who were lost in the war.

Betty's greatest satisfaction is in her relationship with her grandchildren and in their achievements; her youngest grandson was involved with creating a film about the Warsaw ghetto that was so successful it caught the attention and praise of Eli Wiesel; her granddaughters are in college. Betty never spoke with her children about her Holocaust experiences; they never asked about it, but "they felt it," she says. Betty admits that she remained embittered about the Holocaust for many years. But somehow, she says, she was able to come to a kind of truce with it: "I got rid of my anger." Although she has not found comfort in religion, she believes the Holocaust gave some meaning to her life. "We have a responsibility," Betty believes, "because we survived for a reason." When her granddaughter asked Betty to talk to her class at school about her experiences in the Holocaust, she didn't refuse—she was ready.

Betty admits that she is nostalgic for her earlier, happier life, when she was "productive," when the children were young. She misses living in Brooklyn where she could walk to visit both her brother and sister; she remembers happy summers spent in the Catskills, during the prosperous years of the Borscht Belt;[15] taking her children to the theater, or to museums; watching them grow and mature, and trusting them to make constructive decisions about their lives. She keeps busy with daily chores and goes to her community's clubhouse for activities. "Friends take me," she says, to the Jewish Community Center where she is in the advanced Yiddish-speaking group.

Betty's early experiences, she believes, influenced her values, particularly her understanding of how valuable life is; consequently, she's not acquisitive or envious of others. She quotes a Chinese proverb: "An ounce of time is worth more than an ounce of gold." Yet she doesn't fear the passage of time. Betty lives in the moment, she says, adding, "I feel ready for what is coming."

Renee (Renia Felber) Milchberg. I first met Renee at her high-rise condo in Thornhill, a suburb of Toronto, in 2006. We had spoken on the phone a number of times but this was our first face-to-face meeting. After I was greeted with a great hug, as if I were an old friend, we started our conversation over bagels and coffee. Renee's husband, Irving, joined us for a while but soon left so that we could have some privacy. Irving, she told me, had survived the destruction of the ghetto and become a street urchin, one of the "cigarette sellers" in Warsaw during its occupation by the Germans.[16] They had met through mutual friends when Renee was on a trip to Canada. She was impressed with his courage, and she still is; you can sense her pride when she tells his story.

When I asked Renee how she was, she responded, "Basically, I am in good health." Despite her age, it was an unremarkable statement until she recounted some of her medical history. Renee's left arm was left paralyzed by a bout with polio shortly before her town, Sanok, was invaded by the Germans. Ironically, Renee's paralysis may have been one of the reasons for her survival. When Sanok was divided between Germany and the Soviet Union, Renee's mother thought they would be out of harms way on the "Russian side" and left her with friends there while she went back to get Renee's sister. Her mother never returned. Nor did she ever see her sister or grandparents again. It is fairly certain, according to historical accounts of Sanok during that period of the war, that they were deported to Belzec, the death camp. Renee was taken to the city of Lvov by her aunt and uncle and, subsequently, they were deported to Siberia.

In addition to the paralysis, Renee became ill after the war. In 1948, immediately upon her arrival in the United States, she was diagnosed with a lesion on one of her lungs and spent her first year and a half in America at a treatment center in Colorado. Since then she has had occasional health problems, but nothing she considered major. Then, Renee added, she had recently been diagnosed with Parkinson's disease. When we met, her neurologist was still trying out various drugs to control the tremors (fortunately, after a few months, he settled on a treatment that worked). Despite her history Renee, like Irma, has neither the voice nor the attitude of a sick person; she doesn't seem frail or tentative, she is not tense or anxious: quite the contrary, she has a contented and relaxed manner.

While Renee was living at the Girls Club, she decided to attend business school: "I learned how to do one-arm typing so I could get a job." She worked steadily until 1955 when she and Irving married and moved to Niagara Falls, Canada. Renee didn't feel handicapped while she was managing a home and raising two children, or when she worked with her husband in their souvenir shop, within view of the magnificent falls. "It's funny," she said, as if thinking about it for the first time, "I look at other people who have problems and I think they're disabled, but I never thought of myself as disabled."

In Niagara Falls, Renee was active in the sisterhood of their *shul*, and president of the Hadassah chapter. She describes herself as "traditional" in her religious observance—she has always kept a kosher home and attends services during the High Holy Days. On *Yom Kippur*, the day of atonement and abstinence, she participates in the communal *Yizkor* service (an annual memorial prayer service). During this solemn day of prayer and reflection, Renee lights *Yahrzeit* (memorial) candles, participating in one of the mourning rituals that is part of Jewish life. There are many candles—for the family that was lost in the war, as well as the aunt and uncle with whom she traveled to Siberia and Uzbekistan, and with whom she made her way to America. Yet her losses haven't made her relinquish her faith. "God," Renee believes, "had nothing to do with the Holocaust. That was man's doing."

Since they retired, Renee and Irving have been living in Thornhill, a Toronto suburb; her daughter lives nearby and she has many friends there. She is very happy in her spacious and comfortable apartment. "We should have moved sooner," she thinks. The Jewish community in Niagara Falls had dwindled to so few that, she says, "we couldn't get a *minyan* [a quorum of ten men required for a prayer service] anymore; all the older Jews died out and their children had left."

"Nowadays we are slowing down, of course," Renee says. "We used to always drive to Baltimore, to visit my son," a physicist who teaches at the University of Maryland. "We didn't think anything of it; we would take a couple of days and stop on the way. Nowadays, it's too much of a trip. If we go, we fly to Washington, D.C., but that's a trip too." Consequently, her son usually brings Renee's three grandchildren for a long visit in the summer. But if she is "slowing down," she is also "busy all the time, doing nothing." Some of her activities are sedentary; she enjoys crossword puzzles and TV. And she goes out to play cards and to see films.

In addition to her many friends in the Toronto area, Renee also has an active social life in Florida, where she usually spends the winter—several friends there are women she met in Germany after the war, and one who lived at the Girls Club. When I spoke with her recently, Renee and Irving were getting ready to leave for her annual Florida trip. And they were first stopping in Washington, D.C., to spend Thanksgiving with their son and his family. Renee had not gone to Florida the year before due to a setback. She had broken a bone in her foot and, at the same time, re-aggravated an older injury in her shoulder. She wasn't in pain but she was hobbling around awkwardly in a "boot" and needed physical therapy. She expected to fully recover but was feeling vulnerable and wanted to nestle in her home.

Renee has had more than her share of illnesses, but as we have come to understand, aging well means more than being physically well. It also has a great deal to do with attitude and morale—with the ability to remain positive in the face of difficulties. This soft-spoken and gentle woman has been able to do that. She is content with her life, and when she looks back she is able to say, without hesitation: "I made the right choices."

Doris (Dorka Izbicka) Wasserman. Doris, Lucy's childhood friend with whom she was reunited at the Girls Club, recently told me: "Age means nothing. What's important is attitude, your way of thinking. You should not give in to it, as much as possible." Perhaps her view is an exaggeration and a bit of bravado, but it is an example of the type of optimism Vaillant found in those who age well. Doris is one of the elders among the Girls Club women; she was born in 1927 and recently celebrated her eighty-second birthday.

Doris, like some in the Harvard study, found a serious and satisfying creative outlet when she learned that she had a talent for drawing. She had always been skilled in crafts: knitting, needlepoint, sewing. But it wasn't until she retired to what had been her vacation home in Florida that Doris began to take art classes. She discovered her talent for sketching and drawing, particularly for portraiture. Because of glaucoma in her left eye, she hasn't been able to continue this activity over the past couple of years, nor has she been able to read, another of her passions. And, like many elderly, she suffers with back pain. Yet she refuses to complain. "A lot of people *kvetch*" (Yiddish for whine or gripe), she says, "and life is a struggle. Yes, it's not easy," Doris says impatiently, "but you have to learn to live with it, to make the best of it."

Doris and Michael had their wedding reception at the Girls Club more than fifty years ago in a "big beautiful room with a piano"; Lucy was her maid of honor. They settled down in Brooklyn and, when their children were young, she and Lucy used to meet in the park. Doris misses Brooklyn, especially the days when her children were growing up. She looks back upon a good life there—middle-class comfort, summers in a bungalow she owned in the Catskills, some travel. But she is happy in Florida. She and Michael, whose family survived the war years by hiding in a forest in the Ukraine, live in a comfortable villa in a retirement community.

Doris misses being able to "walk out," having all the shops and activities available within walking distance, rather than having to depend on transportation, but the shops are only a short drive from her development. She still drives, although she much prefers to be driven around by her husband, her "private chauffeur." Despite their health problems, he and Doris continue to lead an active life. Doris says: "Compared to others, we're OK. We can go about our business."

Doris has her regular routines and keeps herself busy with shopping, housekeeping, and cooking: "I'm a good cook, but not too big on baking," she admits. She plays cards and engages in activities at the clubhouse. She spends time with a large circle of friends, "some from before." Doris loves having her two sons and their families visit. These days she travels to New Jersey, where her sons and their families live, only for special occasions, such as her grandchildren's *Bat* and *Bar Mitzvot*. Her life does not seem extraordinary until you remember that this woman who possesses such a healthy and positive attitude lost nearly all her family in the Holocaust, that she is a child survivor of the Lodz ghetto—"I am the only survivor from thirty-plus girls in my class," she says; she lived through Auschwitz and Mauthausen. Today she is dealing with serious physical problems. Yet, despite it all, Doris looks back upon her life and sees "beautiful memories."

Fran (Frania Dajcz) Berlin. "When Frania arrived in the Girls Club I didn't know she was alive. We didn't know who survived. How we felt when we met one another and were still breathing!" Lucy said. Although they hadn't met in the Lodz ghetto, Lucy and Fran knew each other because they had traveled the same path through the camps. They became good friends at the Girls Club. But their lives took different directions.

Fran's husband, Seymour, ran a thriving printing business. When their children were young they moved from Brooklyn to Long Island. Fran was involved with Seymour's large extended family and developed a circle of new friends. "My husband was always a good provider," Fran says, "but a workaholic; I had to drag him away." In the "good years," when the children were young, "we would go to Maine in the summer, or go to the Amish country." They traveled in Europe when Fran's daughter was an exchange student in Salzburg. They drove through Austria and Germany, visiting friends she had made in the DP camp. She visited her home town, Pabianice, and Lodz. "I found our old apartment there," she says. In later years, she and Seymour went on cruises.

Fran and Lucy remained in touch for many years. But their contact became sporadic after Seymour retired and the couple moved to a suburb of Santa Fe to be close to their son, who had settled there. The decision to move so far away was not without mixed feelings, Fran said; it was more her husband's and son's decision than hers. She remembers being "heartbroken" when they left New York, and it took several years before she adjusted to living in New

Mexico. But "then I got used to it," she says. "I started seeing positives, the beauty that surrounds me." Over the years, Fran grew to love her large home with its large tract of land and view of the mountains. And she has many friends in Santa Fe, although she quickly qualifies them as acquaintances, not "bosom buddies." They can't replace her old friends, people with whom she's had "friendships for life": European friends she met after the war and women she met in the Girls Club.

For twelve years after she moved to Santa Fe, Fran had the pleasure of being close to her grandson and seeing him grow up. But her son moved to California a few years ago and Fran's daughter lives in Colorado. Her children are not a "continent away," she says, "but they're not nearby either." Now, more than ever, Fran feels very alone and isolated. She spent many years caring for her husband; most of the years, in fact, that she's lived in Santa Fe. But Seymour, who put up a long struggle against cancer, finally succumbed in 2008.

Fran's children have been encouraging her to sell her home and buy a condo in town; they believe it will be easier for their mother to cope. After wisely resisting when it was still too early for her to make another major change in her life, she recently decided to consider the move. But for now, Fran is concentrating on taking care of her physical health, which she says is good. She drives into Santa Fe three times a week to go to the gym. She has lunch with friends from the temple and from Hadassah. She belongs to a reading group. She gardens. She watches TV and is particularly interested in the news. When I spoke with her recently, she was looking forward to a visit from her son and grandson.

Fran is still grieving her loss and is also dealing with "some depression, some sleep problems," but she believes she has the emotional resilience to face the challenges that life as a widow will present.

Finally, another glimpse into the lives of Lucy and Betty (Bronka) as they enter their ninth decade. Predictably, the women are involved in many different kinds of activities, as they have been throughout their lives. But they are also dealing with problems related to their own aging and to the aging of their spouses. There are times they are fearful or depressed, when their thoughts turn to those they lost in the Holocaust. Yet, while they will always grieve for their loved ones, they have been able to keep the past in perspective and have found the optimism to look forward.

According to these and other important criteria, Betty and Lucy are aging well. Despite the trauma and post-traumatic stress which they and all of the women of the Girls Club experienced, Lucy and Betty resist seeing their lives as tragic. The opposite is true. As Lucy says, hardly believing it herself: "We made the American dream out of the ashes of the Holocaust."

Lucy (Lusia Bergman) Pasternak. For the past few years Lucy has been going through a difficult time. It began a couple of years after her husband's retirement. At this writing, Jonas is eighty-eight years old, and while he's in remarkably good physical health, he's been seriously depressed. "His mind is OK," Lucy says, "but he doesn't understand what is happening. It's hard for him to remember who he was."

When Jonas's depression got worse, Lucy sought help from a psychotherapist. Jonas resisted at first; he said that she was using him as an excuse: "I think you need it more," he told her. But he finally agreed and, in fact, they were both helped. In part by talking their problems through, Lucy came to understand that she had to accept Jonas's personality change: "You can't fight it." She decided she'd better start to adjust; she was determined to become kinder to Jonas and to eliminate as much friction and aggravation from their lives as possible. This was a pattern she seems to have followed throughout her married life. Jonas was never easy, "rather demanding," Lucy says. But she is accepting: "You always find some things you can never change in relationships. You have to give it up. Sometime, if you can't make peace with it, you can't go on."

Jonas is somewhat better now, with medication, although he needs a lot of attention and care, which Lucy provides. She says, "I keep him in good health as much as possible. I make sure he eats right"—she consulted a nutritionist—"he eats on time, he gets enough rest, he takes his medicine." Unfortunately, however, Lucy has had some health problems of her own. In addition to some back pain, for which she has had effective physical therapy, she learned that she had cataracts in both of her eyes. Usually the symptoms are apparent long before surgery becomes necessary but "they came on very suddenly," Lucy says. "Before that I didn't know I had anything wrong, or I didn't want to admit it was old age." The first surgery proved to be more complicated and difficult than expected. Lucy was incapacitated and unable to take care of Jonas for several weeks; they stayed with her daughter. The second surgery proved to be easier. But "I was worn out," she said. "I took a long time to come back to myself."

Lucy is recovering her energy, slowly, and resuming a busy schedule. For a time, she said, even though Jonas was having problems with his vision and "his reflexes were not so good," he still drove to their appointments and other activities: "I couldn't take this last thing away from him." But she knows she will someday have to take on the role of driver. Although they're willing, Lucy doesn't want to rely on her children who, she is happy to say, have busy professional and social lives and large families. "I can't ask the kids to give me time off, only when I must, when I have no choice."

Lucy's "homemaking pride is mostly gone now," she says; it's hard to keep up with the demands of home and with Jonas's and her own health issues, including frequent medical appointments. "I'm always busy," she says. Lucy does the shopping, the housekeeping and cooking, and spends a good amount of time taking care of the family finances. Because Jonas was self-employed, he doesn't have a pension, only Social Security. Money is a concern; their high prescription bills run into hundreds more than their drug coverage plan allows.

Lucy's life, like those of the other women, is not ideal in her old age. She is coping with serious problems and doesn't make light of them. But at the same time she says, "We have to go on to do what we can. I do what I can." Lucy doesn't ever consider the alternative—to give up her home, to become dependent upon her children, as caring as they are. "The hardest thing is facing deterioration," she says, yet she doesn't define herself as a sick person. "I'm still OK," she says.

Lucy has been reflecting upon the past: "I have more time to think, and that's not always the best thing, Mourning has gotten worse because I understand more now, I'm more aware. Some things I realize for the first time; before I wouldn't allow myself to get in touch with it." Lucy says that she both lives with the Holocaust every day and, when she looks back on her life, discounts those years because she had no control over what she experienced.

Lucy's personal history, she says, as for all Holocaust survivors, "is divided before the war and after the war." In between, there is a void. "Someone took a whole chunk of years out of our existence. I was suspended in midair, I wasn't on the earth." What enabled her to become sufficiently detached may also have contributed to her ability to survive, and later to recover. Lucy believes that it was her life "before" that gave her the "foundation, and the strength" to heal. Vaillant would agree: "What goes right in childhood predicts the future far better than what goes wrong" (2002, p. 95). Lucy does not believe the Holocaust is a sufficient explanation for the problems many survivors have dealt with, not even her dear friend Sonia: "For me that is so, and I think so for others."

In spite of the difficulties, Lucy believes there are some genuine positives that come with aging. She is not concerned with what she feels are superficial issues that aging women deal with. "Losing your looks? It's not a problem for me. I was pretty and took more care than I do now, but I was never preoccupied with looks, I was not vain." Lucy says she was "naturally unconscious" about her outward appearance. She remembered being particularly aware of this at the wedding of Doris's son: "I looked around at others, at Doris—she is always so put together—and thought I should be more aware of makeup and clothing, but I couldn't do it. Now that I am older I think it was connected to humility." For Lucy, modesty and humility are extremely important values but, at the same time, she's become "bolder." She's more outspoken, more inclined to say what she thinks. Although she would always rather avoid than provoke an argument, she admits: "I say things now I never would before."

Above all, the most positive aspects of her life and her old age are in the *naches*, the pleasure, she takes in watching her family and her grandchildren grow and thrive: "I loved babysitting my grandchildren. I was their second mother, like my grandmother was for me. My greatest joy was when my granddaughter got married. It was a gift from God. Not everyone lives to marry off a granddaughter."

Lucy has arrived at a philosophical view and spiritual peace. She says:

> My life was good and it is still good. I look at others in wheelchairs who can't walk, who have worse conditions, who depend on their children. We go out every day, we can eat what we want, we don't suffer too much physically, we have enough money, even some luxuries.
>
> I do the best I can for my children and grandchildren. The rest I leave to God.

Betty (Bronka Silvering) Berman. Betty was impatient because, like Lucy, she had developed cataracts. Her impatience was because her increasingly blurry vision was interfering with her driving and with her ability to get to her various activities, such as the yoga classes which she says "have kept me sane for the past thirty years. It gets your body in tune, you intuitively relax."

Betty is glad that she decided to have the cataract surgery. It was minor compared with the open heart surgery she'd had in 1989 to correct a condition that had gone undetected until then, but that she probably had had since childhood. With her characteristic energy and determination, she was back to work after six weeks. Today Betty's health, she's relieved to say, is "pretty good, nothing life-threatening." She is able to continue living her very active life.

Still, "it's hard," she says, "coming to terms with mortality. You worry about being alone; and you think more about the past. Not that the Holocaust is more prominent in my thoughts, but I'm freer to talk about it." Betty rarely has nightmares about the war any longer; when the war ended she remembers endlessly "replaying" events in her sleep. "Now I keep the memories in my heart," she says. She doesn't believe she needs formalized rituals of mourning. Nonetheless, she is aware of the impact the Holocaust made upon her life:

> My life was never completely typical; "survivor" was close to the top of the list of my identity. My identity as a survivor has profoundly shaped the course of my life and my world view. Everything in my life is measured against the Holocaust. What effect did it have? Has it taught me to live a good life? To search to be better? How do I compare? But I didn't live my life preoccupied with being a survivor.

Betty is still a docent at the Minneapolis Institute of Art where she started leading tours many decades ago; in 2010 she will have set a record of thirty-five years of volunteer service to the MIA, as it is known locally. Most recently she has been preparing a tour of the MIA's new exhibit of sixty-two objects from the Louvre. And she continues to be the expert in Asian, particularly Chinese, art. But because Betty feels she has much more to learn, she has begun a new project: "I started studying Chinese calligraphy to expand my understanding of Chinese culture. I was always frustrated that I couldn't penetrate the calligraphy; it's always mystified me."

Apart from these activities, Betty gardens for as much of the year as the Minnesota weather allows. She has a very active social life, many friends. She keeps in touch with some of her old friends in New York, and also with Fran. She continues to be an avid reader. She goes to the theater, concerts, films, and lectures. Hy and Betty have always traveled to conferences—he remains involved in his scholarly life as a labor historian—and to visit friends in New York, or their children.

Betty understates her lifelong accomplishments. Looking back she says: "I had a good and interesting life. I did things I wanted to do. Of course there are things I would do differently—but none of the major decisions. And I want to continue to be active, inquiring, learning new things."

Then she sums it all up in a simple statement: "I guess I need another life."

NOTES

1. There is a vast amount of material published on the topic by the National Institute on Aging (NIA), a division of the U.S. National Institutes of Health, which can be found online. Literature is also available from the Alliance for Aging Research. One ongoing study, the Baltimore Longitudinal Study of Aging (BLSA), which began in 1958, was sponsored by the National Institute on Aging.

2. From *As Survivors Age*, Part II 2-5, passim.

3. A notable exception is the Harvard study of adult development, in Vaillant, *Aging Well*, which has been ongoing since the late 1930s.

4. The NIA and others identify subcategories used in their analyses: "young-old," indicating 65–74 years old; "old," 75–84; and "old-old," 85–94. Vaillant, in his discussion of the Harvard project, uses these terms with slightly different ages assigned to them. See Velkoff for estimates of the aging population through the year 2025.

5. The findings relate to the effects of stress on the cellular level, on structures called "telomeres."

6. Hatch is a professor of sociology at the University of Ohio with numerous writings on aging and gender. Her book, *Beyond Gender Differences*, which examines research on aging throughout the life course, is a review and analysis of literature from a wide range of sociological perspectives and contains an extensive bibliography. I agree with her conclusion: The fact that men and women may have to cope with different issues does not support the assertion, by some writers, that one sex does better than the other in adapting to aging. "There is no clear pattern," for supporting that claim; "for every gender role argument," supporting the greater difficulty in "adapting to aging and to life events in older age, the opposite argument has been made" (p. 17).

7. See Dasberg, "Adult child survivor syndrome on deprived childhoods of aging Holocaust survivors." Also Sternberg & Rosenbloom, "Lost Childhood."

8. See Sindler, Wellman, & Stier (p. 189).

9. See David & Pelly, (pp. 51–59) for a detailed discussion.

10. Rosner was explaining the meaning of the title of her book, *Speed of Light*, at the Holocaust Memorial Presentation at SUNY, New Paltz, in 2004.

11. She is on the faculty of the Psychology Department at York University in Toronto.

12. Haas, Helmreich, Sagi-Schwartz et al., Suedfeld, Garner & Nercer, etc. See sources for additional citations.

13. Erikson names eight stages of development, each with its own characteristics, conflicts, and challenges. Resolving the crisis in old age leads to what Erikson called "ego-integrity."

14. Frankl's 1946 book *Man's Search for Meaning* describes his experiences as an inmate, as well as his method of finding a reason to live.

15. "Borscht Belt" is a term used to describe one of the resort areas of the Catskill Mountains in upstate New York, also called the "Jewish Alps." The hotels, bungalow colonies, and *kuchaleyns* (a Yiddish word meaning rented boarding houses in which you "cook for yourself") were the most popular vacation spots for New York Jews in the 1940s through the 1960s, particularly in the summertime. Some of these resorts were originally farms that had been established by Jewish immigrants earlier in the century.

16. See Joseph Ziemian's account, *The Cigarette Sellers of Three Crosses Square*.

Bibliography

Anflick, C. (1999). Resistance: Teen partisans and resisters who fought Nazi tyranny. Eliat, Y. (Series Ed.). *Teen witnesses to the Holocaust.* New York, NY: The Rosen Publishing Group.

Antisemitism in interwar Poland, 1919–1939. (n.d.). Retrieved from http://www .worldfuturefund.org/wffmaster/Reading/Total/Polish%20Antisemitism.htm.

Auschwitz. (2009, May). *Holocaust Encyclopedia.* Retrieved from http://www .ushmm.org/wlc/article.php?ModuleId=10005189.

Axelrod, T. (1999). In the camps: Teens who survived the Nazi concentration camps. Eliat, Y. (Series Ed.). *Teen witnesses to the Holocaust.* New York, NY: The Rosen Publishing Group.

Ayer, E. H. (1999). In the ghettos: Teens who survived the ghettos of the Holocaust. Eliat, Y. (Series Ed.). *Teen witnesses to the Holocaust.* New York, NY: The Rosen Publishing Group.

Baer, E. R. & Goldenberg, M. (Eds.). (2003). *Experience and expression: Women, the Nazis, and the Holocaust.* Detroit, MI: Wayne State University Press.

Barak, Y. (2007, March). The aging of Holocaust survivors: Myth and reality concerning suicide. Ramat Gan, Israel: *The Israel Medical Association Journal (IMAj), 9,* 196–198.

Barak, Y., Alzenberg, D., Szor, H., Swartz, M., Maor, R. & Knobler, H. Y. (2003). Increased suicidal risk amongst aging Holocaust surviviors. *Annals of General Psychiatry, 2 (Suppl 1)*. doi: 10,1186/1475-2832-S1-S151.

Barkan, E. R. (1996). *And still they came: Immigrants and American society, 1920–1990s.* Wheeling, IL: Harlan Davidson.

Bartoszewski, W. (1991). *The convent at Auschwitz.* New York, NY: George Braziller, Inc.

Baskin, J. & Tenenbaum, S. (1994). *Gender and Jewish Studies.* New York, NY: Biblio Press.

Bauer, Y. (2001). *A history of the Holocaust.* Danbury, CT: Franklin Watts.

Bauer, Y. (2002). *Rethinking the Holocaust.* New Haven, CT: Yale University Press.

Baumel, J. T. (1998). *Double jeopardy: Gender and the Holocaust.* Portland, OR: Vallentine-Mitchell.

Bergen-Belsen. (2009, May). *Holocaust Encyclopedia.* Retrieved from http://www .ushmm.org/wlc/article.php?lang=en&ModuleId=10005224.

Bernard, J. (1972). *The children you gave us: A history of 150 years of service to children.* New York, NY: Block.

Bitton-Jackson, L. (1997). *I have lived a thousand years: Growing up in the Holocaust.* New York, NY: Scholastic.

Bitton-Jackson, L. (1980). *Elli: Coming of age in the Holocaust.* New York, NY: Times Books.

Bluegrass, K. (2003). *Hidden from the Holocaust: Stories of resilient children who survived and thrived.* Westport, CT: Praeger Publishing.

Bodnar, J. (1987). *The Transplanted: A history of immigrants in urban America.* Bloomington: Indiana University Press.

Bonanno, G. A. (2004). Loss, trauma, and human resilience: Have we underestimated the human capacity to thrive after articulllely aversive events? *American Psychologist, (59),* 33–41.

Bos, P. R. Women and the Holocaust: Analyzing gender difference. (2003). In E. R. Baer & M. Goldenberg (Eds.), *Experience and expression: Women, the Nazis, and the Holocaust* (pp. 23–52). Detroit, MI: Wayne State University Press.

Browning, C. R. (1993). *The path to genocide.* Cambridge, UK: Cambridge University Press.

Browning, C. R. (2004). *The origins of the final solution: The evolution of Nazi Jewish policy, September 1939–March 1942.* Lincoln: University of Nebraska Press.

Central Commision. "German Crimes in Poland (Warsaw, 1946, 1947) Extermination Camp Chelmno (Kulmhof)." (n.d., n.p). Central Commision for Investigation of German Crimes in Poland. Retrieved from http://weber.ucsd .edu/~lzamosc/gchelmno.html.

Cohen, B. (2007). The children's voice: Postwar collection of testimonies from child survivors of the Holocaust. *Holocaust and Genocide Studies, 21,* 73–95.

Cook, J. M. (2001, Summer). Post-traumatic stress disorder in older adults. *PTSD Research Quarterly, 12* (2), 1–7. Menlo Park, CA: National Center for PTSD.

Danieli, Y. (1988). Treating survivors and children of survivors of the Nazi Holocaust. In F. M. Ochberg (Ed.), *Post-traumatic therapy and victims of violence* (pp. 278–294). New York, NY: Brunner/Mazel.

Danieli, Y. (1992). Preliminary reflections from a psychological perspective. In T. C. van Boven, C. Flinterman, F. Grunfeld, & I. Westendorp (Eds.), *The right to restitution, compensation and rehabilitation for victims of gross violations of human rights and fundamental freedoms.* (Special issue), *12.* Utrecht: Netherlands Institute of Human Rights [Studien Informatiecentrum Mensenrechten], 196–213.

Danieli, Y. (1994, Winter). As survivors age, Part I. *NCP Clinical Quarterly, 4* (1): 1–15. http://www.ncptsd.org/publications/cq/v4/n1/danielia.html.

Danieli, Y. (1994, Spring). As survivors age, Part II. *NCP Clinical Quarterly, 4* (2): 1–11. http://www.ncptsd.org/publications/cq/v4/n2/danielia.html.

Dasberg, H. (2001). Adult child survivor syndrome on deprived childhoods of aging Holocaust survivors. *Israeli Journal of Psychiatry Related Sciences, (38),* 13–26. Jerusalem: AMCHA, National Israeli Center for Psychosocial Support of Holocaust Survivors and the Second Generation.

David, P. & Pelly, S. (Eds.). (2003). *Caring for aging Holocaust survivors: A practice manual.* Toronto: Baycrest Center for Geriatric Care.

Deitrich, S. (2002, July 23). Exhibition dedicated to "forgotten" concentration camp opens. *DW-World-DE Deutsch-Welle.* Retrieved from http://www.dw-world.de/ dw/article/0,2144,2702730,00.html.

Dwork, D. (1991). *Children with a star.* New Haven, CT: Yale University Press.

Eichengreen, L. (1994). *From ashes to life: My memories of the Holocaust.* San Francisco, CA: Mercury House.

Eichengreen, L. (2000). *Rumkowski and the orphans of Lodz.* San Francisco, CA: Mercury House.

Eitinger, L. (1993). The aging Holocaust survivor. Retrieved from http://www .holocaustechoes.com/93etinger2.pdf.

Elkind, D. (1998). *All grown up and no place to go.* (Rev. Ed.). Reading, MA: Perseus Books.

Epstein, J. & Lefkowitz, L. H. (2001). *Shaping losses: Cultural memory and the Holocaust.* Urbana: University of Illinois Press.

Erikson, E. (1959). *Identity and the life cycle* (1980 ed.). New York, NY: Norton.

Erikson, E. & Erikson, J. M. (1997). *The life cycle completed, extended version.* New York, NY: W. W. Norton.

Feigenbaum, A. (1999). The anguish of "liberation." In R. Headland (Ed.), *So others will remember: Holocaust history and survivor testimony.* Montreal, Canada: Vehicule Press. Retrieved from http://www.vehiculepress.com/subjects/jewish/ jewish_holocaust.html.

Fein, Helen (1979) *Accounting for genocide: Victims—and survivors—of the Holocaust.* New York: Free Press.

Fernandes, V. (n.d.). Children and trauma. Retrieved from http://holocaust -children.tripod.com/trauma.html.

Flaum, S. R. (2003). Lodz ghetto deportations and statistics. Retrieved from http:// www.shtetlinks.njewishgen.org/Lodz/statistics.htm.

Flossenbürg Concentration Camp. Retrieved from http://www.holocaust researchproject.org/othercamps/flossenburg.html.

Ford, C. B. (2000). *The girls: Jewish women of Brownsville, Brooklyn, 1940–1995.* Albany: State University of New York Press.

Frankel, B. & Michaels, R. (1951, March). A changing focus in work with young unattached DPs. *The Jewish Social Service Quarterly, 2,* 321–331.

Garner, J. D. & Mercer, S. O. (1989). *Women as they age: Challenge, opportunity, and triumph.* New York, NY: Haworth Press.

Giddens, S. (1999). Escape: Teens who escaped the Holocaust to freedom. Eliat, Y. (Series Ed.). *Teen witnesses to the Holocaust.* New York: The Rosen Publishing Group.

Gilligan, C. (1982). *In a different voice: Psychological theory and women's development.* Cambridge, MA: Harvard University Press.

Greene, R. R. (2005, July 13). Holocaust survivors: A study in resilience. Reprinted from the *Journal of Gerontological Social Work, 37* (1). *If Not Now* (e-journal), pp. 1–20. Retrieved from http://www.baycrest.org.

Greenglass, E. R. (2002, Winter). Holocaust survivors, coping and well-being. *If Not Now* (e-journal). Retrieved from http://www.baycrest.org.Article2.

Hart, K. (1982). *Return to Auschwitz: The remarkable life of a girl who survived the Holocaust.* New York, NY: Atheneum.

Hass, A. (1996a). *The Aftermath: Living with the Holocaust.* New York, NY: Cambridge University Press.

Hass, A. (1996b). *In the shadow of the Holocaust: The second generation.* New York, NY: Cambridge University Press.

Hatch, L. R. (2000). *Beyond gender differences: Adaptation to aging in life course perspective.* Amityville, NY: Baywood Publishing.

Helmreich, W. B. (1992). *Against all odds: Holocaust survivors and the successful lives they made in America.* New York, NY: Simon & Schuster.

Hemdinger, J. & Krell, R. (2000). *The children of Buchenwald: Child survivors of the Holocaust and their post-war lives.* Jerusalem, Israel: Gefen.

Here and Now: The vision of the Jewish labor Bund in interwar Poland. (2002, October). Exhibition at the YIVO Institute for Jewish Research. Retrieved from http://www.yivo.org/digital_exhibitions/index.php?mcid=72&oid=10.

Herman, J. L. (1992). *Trauma and recovery: The aftermath of violence from domestic abuse to political terror.* New York, NY: Basic Books.

Isaacson, J. M. (1990). *Seed of Sarah: Memoirs of a survivor.* Urbana: University of Illinois Press.

Judt, T. (2008). The "problem of evil" in postwar Europe. *New York Review of Books, 55* (2), 33–35.

Katz, E. & Ringleheim, J. (Eds.). (1983). Proceedings of the Conference on Women Surviving the Holocaust, Stern College, New York, NY. *Occasional papers from the Institute for Research in History.* New York, NY: Institute for Research in History.

Kestenberg, J. S. & Brenner, I. (1996). *The last witness: The child survivor of the Holocaust.* Washington, DC: American Psychiatric Press.

Kestenberg, J. S. & Kahn, C. (1998). *Children surviving persecution: An international study of trauma and healing.* Westport, CT: Praeger.

Kleinberg, S. (1980). *Alienated affections: Being gay in America.* New York: St. Martin's Press.

Kleinberg, S. (2002). *The fugitive self.* United States: Exlibris Corporation.

Kreisler, H. (1999, November 2). Evil, the self, and survival: Conversation with Robert J. Lifton, M.D. *Conversations with History.* Berkeley, CA: Institute of International Studies. Retrieved from http://globetrotter.berkeley.edu/people/ Lifton/lifton-con3.html.

Krell, R. (1993). Child survivors of the Holocaust: Strategies of adaptation. *Canadian Journal of Psychiatry, 38,* 384–389.

Kustanowitz, E. (1999). The hidden children of the Holocaust: Teens who hid from the Nazis. Eliat, Y. (Series Ed.). *Teen witnesses to the Holocaust.* New York, NY: The Rosen Publishing Group.

Leitner, I. & Leitner, I. A. (1985). *Saving the fragments: From Auschwitz to New York.* New York, NY: New American Library.

Leland, J. (2008, November 8). Once just a sign of aging, falls merit complex care. *The New York Times,* p. A1.

Levin, N. (1993). *The destruction of European Jewry.* New York, NY: Schocken Books.

Lewin, R. G. (Ed.). (1990). *Witnesses to the Holocaust: An oral history.* New York, NY: Simon & Schuster/Twayne.

Liebster, S. A. (2000). *Facing the lion: Memoirs of a young girl in Nazi Europe.* New Orleans, LA: Grammaton Press.

Linden, R. R. (1993). *Making stories, making selves: Feminist reflections on the Holocaust.* Columbus: Ohio State University Press.

Lisciotto, C., Webb, C. & McConney, S. (2008). Flossenburg Concentration Camp. Retrieved from http://www.holocaustresearchproject.org/othercamps/flossenburg .html.

Lodz. *Holocaust Encyclopedia.* (2009, May). Retrieved from http://www.ushmm.org/ wlc/article.php?lang=en&ModuleId=10005071.

Marcus, J. M. (1983). *Social and political history of the Jews in Poland, 1919–1939.* New York, NY: Mouton Publishers.

Marks, J. (1995). *The hidden children: The secret survivors of the Holocaust.* Toronto: Bantam Books.

Mendelsohn, D. (2008, November 3). Stolen suffering. *New York Times.* Retrieved from http://www.nytimes.com/2008/03/09/opinion/9mendelsohn.html.

Modai, I. (1994). Forgetting childhood: A defense mechanism against psychosis in a Holocaust survivor. *Clinical Gerontologist, 14* (3), 67–71.

Moseley, Marcus. (2001, Spring/Summer) "Life, literature: Autobiographies of Jewish youth in interwar Poland." *Jewish Social Studies, 7, 3.*

Moskovitz, S. & Krell, R. (1990). Child survivors of the Holocaust: Psychological adaptations to survival. *Israel Journal of Psychiatry and Related Services, 27* (2), 81–91.

Neumann, A. (1998, Winter). On experience, memory, and knowing: A post-Holocaust (auto)biography. *Curriculum Inquiry, 28* (4), 425–442.

Nicholas, L. H. (2005). *Cruel world: The children of Europe in the Nazi web.* New York, NY: Knopf.

Normal Aging. (2009). *Research for a New Age, NIH Publication No. 93-1129.* Baltimore Longitudinal Study of Aging. National Institute on Aging/National Institutes of Health, 1–7. Retrieved from http://www.healthandage.com/html/min/nih/content/booklets/research_new_age/page3.htm.

Nowak, S. (2003). Ruptured lives and shattered beliefs: A feminist analysis of *Tikkun Atzmi* in Holocaust literature. In E. R. Baer & M. Goldenberg (Eds.), *Experience and expression: Women, the Nazis, and the Holocaust* (pp. 180–200). Detroit, MI: Wayne State University Press.

Ofer, A. & Weitzman, L. J. (1998). *Women in the Holocaust.* New Haven: Yale University Press.

On this day. 1945: British troops liberate Bergen-Belsen. *BBC News archive WWII and 1950–2005.* Retrieved from http://news.bbc.co.uk/onthisday/hi/dates/stories/april/15/newsid_3557000/3557341.stm.

Pasternak, J. (n.d.). *The tragedy of the Tornopol Jews: Diary by Jonas Pasternak.* (Bergman, E., Trans.). Unpublished manuscript.

Peremyshlyany: Town in Western Ukraine. Retrieved from Pdrehttp://www
.personal.ceu.hu/students/97/Roman_Zakharii/peremyshlyany.htm.

Perl, L. & Lazan, M. B. (1996). *Four perfect pebbles: A Holocaust story.* New York,
NY: Avon Books.

Plight of Jewish children. (2009, May 4). *Holocaust Encyclocpedia.* Retrieved from
http://www.ushmm.org/wlc/article.php?lang=en&ModuleId=10006124.

Podolska, J. (2004a, August). *Exhibition: The children of the Lodz ghetto* (Olejnik, I.,
Trans.). Lodz, Poland: Bilbo.

Podolska, J. (2004b). *Traces of the Litzmannstadt-getto: A guide to the past.* (Dekiert,
D., Trans.). Lodz, Poland: Pia,tek Trzynastego.

Polonsky, A., Mendelsohn, E. & Tomaszewsk, J. (Eds.). (1994). *Polin: Studies in
Polish Jewry, Volume 8. Jews in independent Poland, 1918–1939.* Oxford, UK:
Littman Library of Jewish Civilization.

Prazmowska, A. (2001). Fallout from the War: Antisemitism in Poland. *Poland's
century: War, communism and anti-Semitism.* London School of Economics and
Political Science. Retrieved from http://www.fathom.com/course/72809602/
session2.html.

Rabinowicz, H. M. (1965). *The legacy of Polish Jewry: A history of Polish Jews in the
inter-war years, 1919–1939.* New York, NY: T. Yoseloff.

Rabinowitz, D. (1976). *New lives: Survivors of the Holocaust living in America.* New
York, NY: Knopf.

Ringleheim, J. (1998). The split between gender and the Holocaust. In Ofer, A. & L.
J. Weitzman, *Women in the Holocaust* (pp. 340–351). New Haven: Yale University
Press.

Rittner, C. & Roth, J. K. (Eds.). (1993). *Different voices: Women and the Holocaust.*
St. Paul, MN: Paragon House.

Rockman, P. (n.d.). Issues of interviewing people with painful childhood memories:
Child survivors of the Holocaust and the stolen children. *Descendants of the
Shoah.* Retrieved from http://www.dosinc.org.au/stories8.html.

Rohozinska, J. (2000, January). A complicated coexistence: Polish-Jewish relations
through the centuries. *Central Europe Review, 2* (4). Retrieved from http://www
.pecina.cz/files/www.ce-review.org/00/4/rohozinska4.html.

Rosenbaum, T. (2002, October 12). The survivor who survived. *The New York Times*. Retrieved from http://www.query,nytimes.com/gst/fullpae.html.

Rosenthal, G. (2003, December). The healing effects of storytelling: On the conditions of curative storytelling in the context of research and counseling. *Qualitative Inquiry, 9* (6), 915–933.

Rosner, E. (2004, April 20). Turning sorry into song: The Holocaust in memory and art. Presented at the Holocaust Memorial observance. Department of Jewish Studies, State University of New York at New Paltz.

Roth, J. K. (2003). Equality, neutrality, particularity: Perspectives on women and the Holocaust. In E. R. Baer & M. Goldenberg (Eds.), *Experience and expression: Women, the Nazis, and the Holocaust* (pp. 5–22). Detroit, MI: Wayne State University Press.

Sagi-Schwartz, A., Ijzendoorn, M. H., Grossman, K. E., Joels, T., Grossmann, K., Sharf, M. & Alkalay, S. (2003, June). Attachment and traumatic stress in female Holocaust child survivors and their daughters. *American Journal of Psychiatry, 160* (6), 1086–1092.

Salamon, A. (n.d). Liberation and beyond, freed at last. *Childhood in times of war.* Chapter 5, part 3: Retrieved from http://www.remember.org/jean/index.html.

Salsitz, N. (2002). (With S. Kaish). *Three homelands: Memories of a Jewish life in Poland, Israel and America.* Syracuse, NY: Syracuse University Press.

Seidman, I. E. (1998). *Interviewing as qualitative research: A guide for researchers in education and the social sciences* (2nd ed.). New York, NY: Teachers College Press.

Shandler, J. (2002). *Awakening lives: Autobiographies of Jewish youth in Poland before the Holocaust.* New Haven, CT: Yale University Press.

Sharbit. E. (Ed.). (2001). Memorial book of Sanok and vicinity (Poland): 49°34' / 22°12'. In S. Spector (Ed.) & G. Wigider (Consulting Ed.), *The encyclopedia of Jewish life before and during the Holocaust.* Jerusalem, Israel: Yad Vashem. Retrieved from http://www.shtetlinks.jewishgen.org/Sanok/.

Sindler, A. J., Wellman, N. S. & Stier, O. B. (2004, April). Holocaust survivors report long-term effects on attitudes toward food. *Journal of Nutrition Education and Behavior, 36*, 189.

Slawomir, G. & Podgursky, R. (Producers and Directors). (2007). *Saved by deportation: An unknown odyssey of Polish Jews.* [Motion Picture] Ithaca, NY: Log In Productions.

Society and Aging. (2009). *Research for a New Age, NIH Publication No. 93-1129.* Baltimore Longitudinal Study of Aging. National Institute on Aging/National Institutes of Health (NIA/NIH), 1–10. Retrieved from http://www.healthandage .com/html/min/nih/content/booklets/research_new_age/page5.htm#start.

Speilberg, S. (Producer) & Moll, J. (Director). (2002, November). *The Last Days* [Motion Picture] United States: Universal Studios.

Stargardt, N. (2006). *Witnesses to War.* New York, NY: Knopf.

Stein, A. (1994). *Hidden children: Forgotten survivors of the Holocaust.* Harmondsworth, Middlesex, UK: Penguin Books.

Stein, R. (2004, November 30). Study is first to confirm that stress speeds aging. *The Washington Post*, p. A1.

Steinlauf, M. C. (2002). Jewish politics and youth culture in interwar Poland: Preliminary evidence from the YIVO autobiographies. In Z. Gitelman (Ed.), *The emergence of modern Jewish politics: Bundism and Zionism in Eastern Europe* (pp. 95–106). Pittsburgh, PA: University of Pittsburgh Press.

Sternberg, M. & Rosenbloom, M. (2000, February). Lost childhood—Lessons from the Holocaust: Implications for adult adjustment. *Child and Adolescent Social Work Journal, 17,* 5–17.

Subgoal 1: Unlock the Secrets of Aging, Health, and Longevity. (2001, May). National Institute on Aging, NIH Publication No. 01-4951. Retrieved from http:// www.nia.nih.gov/NR/rdonlyres/E6765778-B533-44BB-9774 -1FB6821B1A14/2696/niasp.pdf-09-26-2009.

Suedfeld, P. (2001). *Life from the ashes: Social science careers of young Holocaust refugees and survivors.* Ann Arbor: University of Michigan Press.

Suedfeld, P. (2002, January 24). Life after the ashes: The postwar pain, and resilience of young Holocaust survivors (pp. 1–24). Monna and Otto Weinmann Lecture Series. Washington, DC: United States Holocaust Memorial Museum, Center for Advanced Studies.

Tarnopol, 49°33' / 25°35'. (1980). In *Encyclopedia of Jewish Communities in Poland, Volume II.* (Polin, P. H., Trans.). Jerusalem, Israel: Yad Vashem.

Tec, N. (2003). *Resilience and courage: Women, men and the Holocaust.* New Haven, CT: Yale University Press.

Tito, E. T. (1999). Liberation: Teens in the concentration camps and the teen soldiers who liberated them. Eliat, Y. (Series Ed.). *Teen witnesses to the Holocaust.* New York: The Rosen Publishing Group.

United States policy toward refugees, 1941–1952. (2009, May). *Holocaust Encyclopedia.* Retrieved from http://www.ushmm.org/wlc/article.php?lang=en&ModuleId=10007094.

Vaillant, G. E. (2002). *Aging well: Surprising guideposts to a happier life from the landmark Harvard study of adult development.* Boston, MA: Little, Brown.

Velkoff, V. A., & Lawson, V. A. (1998, December). Gender and aging: Caregiving. U.S. Department of Commerce, Economics and Statistics Administration. Bureau of the Census: 1–7. Retrieved from http://www.census.gov/ipc/prod/ib-9803.pdf.

Weiner, R. (2010). Bergen-Belsen. Jewish Virtual Library: American-Israeli Cooperative Enterprise. Retrieved from http://www.jewishvirtuallibrary.org/jsource/Holocaust/Belsen.html.

Wilkomirski, B. (1995). *Fragments: Memories of a wartime childhood.* (Janeway, C. B., Trans.). New York, NY: Schocken Books.

Women's Health. (2009). *Research for a New Age, NIH Publication No. 93-1129.* Baltimore Longitudinal Study of Aging. National Institute on Aging/National Institutes of Health (NIA/NIH), 1–9. Retrieved from http://www.healthandage.com/html/min/nih/content/booklets/research_new_age/page6.htm#start.

Wyman, M. (1998). *DPs: Europe's displaced persons, 1945–1951.* Ithaca, NY: Cornell University Press.

Zeilsheim. (2009, May). *Holocaust Encyclopedia.* Retrieved from http://www.ushmm.org/museum/exhibit/online/dp/camp14.htm.

Ziemian, J. (1977). *The cigarette sellers of Three Crosses Square.* (David, J., Trans.). New York, NY: Avon.

Zimmerman, J. D. (Ed.). (2003). *Contested memories: Poles and Jews during the Holocaust and its aftermath.* New Brunswick, NJ: Rutgers University Press.

Zuckerman, A. (1991). *A voice in the chorus: Memories of a teenager saved by Schindler.* Stamford, CT: Longmeadow Press.

Index

About the Author

Carole Bell Ford, professor emerita at Empire State College, at the State University of New York, holds a master's degree in history (State University of New York) and a doctorate in education history (Teachers College, Columbia University). She taught historical and women's studies throughout a forty-year academic career. Upon her retirement from the college, she turned her attention to writing. Her previous books include *The Girls: Jewish Women of Brownsville, Brooklyn* (2000) and *The Women of Court Watch: Reform of a Corrupt Family Court* (2005). Carole and her husband, Steve, reside in New Paltz, New York.

LaVergne, TN USA
08 September 2010
196390LV00004B/8/P